Instructor's Manual to accompany

VISIONS ACROSS THE AMERICAS

Short Essays for Composition

Third Edition

J. STERLING WARNER
Evergreen Valley College

Judith Hilliard
San Jose State University

VINCENT PIRO
Merced College

ESL PROGRAM
BROWARD COMMUNITY COLLEGE
JUDSON A. SAMUELS
SOUTH CAMPUS
7200 HOLLYWOOD/PINES BOULEVARD
PEMBROKE PINES, FL 33024

HARCOURT
BRACE

HARCOURT BRACE COLLEGE PUBLISHERS

Fort Worth   Philadelphia   San Diego   New York   Orlando   Austin   San Antonio
Toronto   Montreal   London   Sydney   Tokyo

ISBN: 0-15-505225-X

Address for Editorial Correspondence:
Harcourt Brace College Publishers
301 Commerce Street, Suite 3700
Fort Worth, TX 76102

Address for Orders:
Harcourt Brace and Company
6277 Sea Harbor Drive
Orlando, FL 32887
1-800-782-4479, or 1-800-433-0001 (in Florida)

Printed in the United States of America

7 8 9 0 1 2 3 4 5 6 023 9 8 7 6 5 4 3 2 1

Contents

iii

I. Pronunciation Guide to Authors' Names

AUTHORS' NAMES	PRONUNCIATION
Pat Mora	PAT MORE-AH
Joanne Jaime	JOE-ANN JAY-ME
Peter Elbow	PEA-TER ELL-BOW
Toni Morrison	TOE-KNEE MORE-ESS-SON
Amy Tan	A-ME TAN
Ray Bradbury	RAY BRAD-BURY
Louise Erdrich	LOU-EASE ERD-RICH
Maxine Hong Kingston	MAKS-EEN HONG KING-STON
Black Elk	BLACK ELK
Alice Walker	AL-ISS WAH-KER
Nguyen Ngoc Ngan	WHEN KNOCK NON
Toshio Mori	TOE-SHE-OH MORE-EE
Maya Angelou	MY-AH AN-GE-LOU
Russell C. Leong	RUSS-ELL CEE LEH-UNG
Katherine Barrett	KATH-ER-INN BEAR-IT
N. Scott Momaday	EN SCOT MOM-AH-DAY
Barbara Graham	BAR-BAH-RAH GREY-HAM
Jack Kroll	JACK KUH-ROLL
Nikki Giovanni	NICK-EE GEE-OH-VON-EE
Philip K. Chiu	FILL-UP KAY CHEW
Barbara Mikulski	BAR-BAH-RAH MI-KULL-SKI
Stephanie Ericsson	STEH-FAN-EE ERR-EEK-SON
Isaac Asimov	EYE-SICK AS-EH-MAUVE
Jo Goodwin Parker	JOE GOOD-WIN PAR-KUR
Guillermo Gómez-Peña	GEY-YAIR-MO GO-MEZ PAIN-YA
Jane and Michael Stern	JAYN and MY-KELL STERN
Richard Rodriguez	RICH-ERD ROD-REE-GUSS
Garrison Keillor	GAIR-EH-SON KEY-LORE
Joyce Jarrett	JOYCESS JAIR-IT
Malcolm X	MAL-COME EX
Luiz Valdez	LOU-EASE VALL-DEZ
Jessica Mitford	JESS-EE-KAH MITT-FORD
Andrew Lam	AN-DREW LAMB
Suzanne Britt	SUE-ZAN BRIT
Ursula Le Guin	ERR-SAW-LAH LAH GWIN
Michael T. Kaufman	MY-KELL TEE COUGH-MAN
E. B. White	EE BEE WHITE

AUTHORS' NAMES	PRONUNCIATION
Martin Luther King, Jr.	MAR-TIN LOO-THUR KING
Constance García-Barrio	CON-STANCE GAR-C-UH BAR-EE-O
Robertson Davies	RAW-BERT-SON DAY-VEES
Gary Tewalestewa	GAIR-EE TE-WALL-EH-STAH-WA
Robert Bly	RAW-BERT BLY
Megan McGuire	MAY-GUN MAC-GWIRE
Karen Ray	KAIR-UN RAY
Allene Guss Grognet	AL-LEAN GUSS GROG-NET
Carlos Bulosan	KAR-LOWS BUGH-LOW-SAHN
Jeanne Wakatsuki Houston	JEEN WA-KA-TSU-KEY HYOU-STON
Dorothy Parker	DOOR-OH-THEEY PAR-KUR
Frank LaPeña	FRANK LAH PAIN-YA
Cynthia Lopez	SIN-THEE-AH LOW-PEZ
Reginald Lockett	REH-GIN-OLD LOCK-IT
Woody Allen	WOOD-EE AL-LEN
Barbara Ehrenreich	BAR-BAH-RAH AIR-IN-WRICK
Paula Gunn Allen	PAW-LAH GUN AL-LEN
Imamu Amiri Baraka	EE-MAH-MOO AH-MERE-EE BAH-RAH-KAH
Judy Christrup	JEW-DEE KRIST-RUP
Mark Charles Fissel	MARK CHAR-ELS FISS-ELL
Douglas Laycock	DUG-LESS LAY-KOK
Gore Vidal	GORE VEE-DOLL
Phyllis McGinley	FILL-US MAK-GIN-LAY
Michael Dorris	MY-KELL DOOR-ISS
Ron Glass	RAWN GLASS
Kim Stanley Robinson	KIM STAN-LEE ROB-IN-SON
Rose Anna Higashi	ROSE AN-AH HUH-GAW-SHE
Louise Erdrich	LOU-EASE ERD-RICH
Edwin Arlington Robinson	ED-WIN ARE-LING-TON ROB-IN-SON
Janice Mirikitani	JAN-ESS MIR-RA-KA-TAN-EE
Jocelyn S. Young	JAW-SAW-LYNN ESS YOUNG
Mark Nicholl-Johnson	MARK NICKEL-JOHN-SON

II. Using the Instructor's Manual

To make the Instructor's Manual for the Third Edition of *Visions Across the Americas* more of a resource text than an answer key, we have included some instructor-oriented essays: Jocelyn S. Young's: "Integrating Technology into the Writing Process" and Mark Nicholl-Johnson's: "Variations on Writing Assignments." Also, in response to the many individuals who requested additional short-answer writing exercises, we have included a selected batch of quizzes—quizzes based on readings in the text. Many of these quizzes move beyond a simple query about an essay's content or developmental strategies into questions about the valuable role of vocabulary in communication.

For your convenience, we have placed no more than one quiz per page so that you might photocopy them for classroom use. We waive copyright restrictions to reprint selected quizzes—as well as the Selected Bibliography of Multicultural Literature—when—AND ONLY WHEN—they are used in class; otherwise, all copyright restrictions for reprint permission apply.

As in the first two IMs for *Visions Across the Americas,* with the exception of Chapter 1: "Communicating Is Language at Work," this manual offers at least two different classroom approaches for teaching each of the rhetorical modes before supplying answers to the Post-reading apparatus in this text. While the nature of each approach may vary from being innovative to conventional, our intention is to emphasize neither as more preferable than the other. Instead, we want to offer instructors a number of different methods of achieving the same objective in the composition classroom. The suggested methods to teaching a rhetorical mode, when synthesized with the way one usually teaches a class, will hopefully provide an instructor with a renewed perspective of the composition process—an invigorating, fresh perspective that will benefit both teacher and the recipient of his or her information: the student. Many of the following approaches include visual aids for the students (e.g., words on the blackboard, whiteboard, or overhead projectors).

Though not always mentioned specifically, most exercises involving some sort of visual aid work equally well in a computer-assisted writing classroom. For instance, instead of writing a word on the blackboard, an instructor might use a complete computer network to send sentences, paragraphs, or stimulus words to each student's terminal. Then, the class would proceed with the suggested exercises with the ability to interface each other's terminal. With an LC panel, instructors could also project materials on a screen.

In addition to classroom approaches to rhetorical modes and suggested answers for the Post-reading apparatus on "Content" and "Strategies and Structures," we have once again included a set of poems followed by the same apparatus found with the essays in our text. Finally, we have also updated our brief bibliography of multicultural literature which you can integrate into your present reading list or use to devise such a list from scratch. Granted our compilation of authors and their contributions to literature remains more "representative" than "exhaustive." Nonetheless, we think you will agree, our bibliography can be a valuable resource, for it clearly identifies some of the fine literature (specifically, short stories, novels, and poetry) that has been written in the last century by people from diverse, exciting cultures.

III. Approaches to Rhetorical Modes and Suggested Answers for Post-reading Questions

Communicating Is Language at Work

Approaches to Language at Work: For a detailed look at approaches to teaching the reading and/or writing process, see the introduction to Chapter One. (The first two essays in Chapter One are annotated in the main text.)

TONI MORRISON

WRITERS TOGETHER

Annotated in the textbook.

PETER ELBOW

FREEWRITING

CONTENT

1. Freewriting is when the author composes something nonstop without concern for grammatical or mechanical correctness; it can be unfocused or focused and often is used to explore topics. It is a way of generating ideas. One begins by making "words, whatever they are. . . ."

2. Elbow feels that writers edit too early in the writing process.

3. When one freewrites, one is not worried about the end product. One is not concerned with making mistakes which can inhibit the creative process.

4.   Premature editing causes the writer to become *nervous, jumpy, inhibited,* and *incoherent.*

STRATEGIES AND STRUCTURES

1.   Elbow's example illustrates how almost anything is acceptable in freewriting. Freewriting has no definite form or shape, just whatever is on the writer's mind.

2.   By his use of common language, Elbow comes across as a sincere individual, talking neither above nor below his audience. He is a real person who is not pretentious; therefore, he is more trustworthy.

3.   Since excessive editing can be one of the major stumbling blocks in the early stages of the writing process, Elbow feels it is necessary to emphasize the creative rather than the mechanical process of writing.

JOANNE JAIME

MARRIAGE: A CHANGING INSTITUTION

Annotated in the textbook.

PAT MORA

WHY I AM A WRITER

CONTENT

1.   Mora writes for several reasons: because she reads, she likes to express herself, she likes to hear "voices of people" she will never know, and she is curious. In addition, she writes because it is a way of saving her feelings. Most importantly, she writes because she is Hispanic and believes "that Hispanics need to take their rightful place in American literature." Ultimately, she states "she writes to try to correct . . . images of worth" which have hurt the images of Hispanics and others.

2.   On one hand, she takes pleasure in writing and in her ability to express herself. On the other hand, she is always a bit dissatisfied with her writing.

3. Mora did not speak Spanish in school because she did not want to be different from the mainstream people who thought speaking Spanish was "odd."

4. One way Mora tends to correct images of worth through her writing is to perpetuate pride in one's cultural roots. As such, one can be himself or herself and not be subject to stereotypes (such as, "thin, blond, and rich, rich, rich"). Students may also identify other ways that Mora corrects images.

STRATEGIES AND STRUCTURES

1. Mora tells how she did not speak Spanish in school so that she would fit in. This personal example acts as an illustration of not wanting to be different from others. The author gives several short examples of the unimportant things: cars, houses, the color of a person's skin, and the languages that people speak at home.

2. Each topic sentence identifies the main idea of the paragraphs and helps focus the paragraph for the reader. By placing a topic sentence at the beginning of each paragraph, the author leads the reader carefully from example to example.

3. Mora begins many of the paragraphs with "I write" which brings a great deal of coherence and unity to the essay. Answers will vary to the second part of the question.

4. In both the first and last paragraph, the focus is upon people. Mora begins her essay saying "I like people," discusses why she has had occasional feelings of inferiority, but concludes asserting herself as an individual: she will "take pride in being a Hispanic writer" and "will continue to write and to struggle to say what no other writer can say in quite the same way."

RAY BRADBURY

THE JOY OF WRITING

CONTENT

1. The main point of "The Joy of Writing" is that authors must approach their writing with "zest" and "gusto." In addition, they must write with a *fire* about topics which they "love" or "hate."

2. Answers will vary here. You might point out, however, that Bradbury does not include any women or ethnic writers in his list of great au-

thors, artists, and musicians. Ask the class if the omission of writers outside the classical literary canon detracts from the effectiveness of this article. (You might want to take this opportunity to discuss what is meant by a "literary canon.")

3. Bradbury implies that words have the power to light fires—to challenge a "cherished prejudice" so that "it slammed the page like a lightning bolt." Another way of looking at this would be that words have the power to create, as well as destroy. Artists of all kinds have ". . . seized a bit of the quicksilver of life, froze[n] it for all time. . . ."

4. Answers will vary here. However, we suggest that you take the time to point out that by looking for the "little loves and bitternesses" in life, they can then be formed into words and transferred to paper.

STRATEGIES AND STRUCTURES

1. Bradbury appeals to the two most basic instincts in the world—love and hate—in "The Joy of Writing." He asks us to bring these instincts to the surface and use them to stimulate our creative processes. In other words, Bradbury encourages all authors to draw from innate passions in order to project material with "zest" and "gusto."

2. Bradbury's insight that writing is ". . . almost like a weather report: hot today, cool tomorrow," points out an essential understanding people should have about writing. He suggests than an author's first draft of an essay or story should be written with "fire," but on subsequent days, he or she must pour "critical water on the simmering coals," in order to clearly and effectively revise and edit the piece. You might ask students to compare Bradbury's advice about enjoying the fire of a first draft to what Peter Elbow says about *freewriting*. Both encourage unrestrained invention, prior to the process of revising and editing. As Elbow says, "The habit of compulsive, premature editing doesn't just make writing hard. It makes writing dead." Bradbury would no doubt agree because a person who prematurely begins to edit will have never reveled in the "fire" of a first draft.

3. By showing us how he thinks, Bradbury illustrates a creative mind at work. For instance, when he was leafing through a copy of *Harper's Bazaar* at his dentist's office, he became so enraged at some photographs that used "Puerto Rican backstreets as props" that he left the office, went home immediately, and wrote the story "Sun and Shadow" which was a "story of an old Puerto Rican who ruins the *Bazaar* photographer's afternoon by sneaking into each picture and dropping his pants."

4. "Zest" and "gusto" encompass the various emotions Bradbury says should be an integral part of every essay or story. By beginning his

essay with these key words, developing what he means by them in the body of his essay, and concluding his essay by referring to them, Bradbury drives home his belief that enlisting one's passions when composing the first draft of an essay or story is essential. To do otherwise would be to miss out on "the fun of anger and disillusion, the fun of loving and being loved, of moving and being moved by this masked ball which dances us from the cradle of churchyard."

AMY TAN

My Mother's English

CONTENT

1. Tan's essay demonstrates the prejudices and injustices her mother encountered because of the way she spoke. However, Tan also illustrates how her mother's English was even more powerful and "to the point" than proper English (e.g., her encounter with the stockbroker).

2. Tan speaks of several situations wherein she varies the sort of English she uses: standard English (when she talks to the stockbroker and the doctor), and broken English (when she talks with her mother and husband).

3. Amy Tan's friends often find her mother difficult to understand. Doctors, lawyers, and other professionals seem to think that her mother's imperfect English indicates a low level of intelligence. For this reason, Tan was initially embarrassed by the English her mother spoke. Later, however, she finds her mother's English: "vivid, direct, full of observation and imagery."

4. The author impersonates her mother on the telephone to hide the latter's broken English—and its limitations. Tan does this because when her mother speaks in public, she is often ignored or not taken seriously.

STRATEGIES AND STRUCTURES

1. The opening paragraph established that Tan is an expert with language: it is the tool of her trade, and it also introduces the topic of her use of many Englishes and alludes to the influential force behind them—her mother.

2. She illustrates her mother's use of vivid language—full of observation and imagery—by giving direct quotes from her mother's

speech. For instance, in her description of Du Zong, she gives a vivid portrait of a Chinese gangster.

3. First, she comments that others ignore her mother when she speaks. Through the use of statistics she shows that very few people understand her mother, e.g., some can understand only 50 percent of what her mother says, others 80 percent.

4. It is obvious that authority figures must deal with her mother's direct language, which demands a response and does not allow one to "beat around the bush."

NARRATION

APPROACHES TO NARRATION

1. To introduce the concept of chronology, have students arrange a series of pictures in chronological order and explain why they arranged the pictures as they did.

2. The instructor should begin class by telling an unusual story. Then have the students write their versions of what the teacher said. You can then use these different accounts to teach the oral tradition by asking what common elements appeared in each story and how each version differed.

MAXINE HONG KINGSTON
GHOSTS

CONTENT

1. Answers will vary.

2. Kingston defines heroes as big eaters who enter into combat against supernatural elements without fear. Modern American heroes tend to acquire great material wealth, are leaders, and are successful. One common element in both cultures is that heroes are winners.

3. Her mother and other heroes defeat the ghosts because they do not give up. The heroes have a variety of ways of defeating the ghosts, but one common element is that they eat these supernatural beings.

4. The author brings in Chinese names and words to give her story authenticity, indicating a definite cultural heritage.

STRATEGIES AND STRUCTURES

1. She obtains specific information about ghosts from the stories she heard from her mother, and from her own research.

2. She gives detailed descriptions of several battles with ghosts.

3. Kingston's reverse chronology allows her to save the most fantastic story until the end.

4. The author uses words such as when, another, the first time, after that, once, when, and the next to guide the reader.

5. Kingston illustrates heroism through the use of specific examples: Kao Chung, Chou Yi-Han, Chen Luan-Feng, and Wei Pang.

BLACK ELK

THE OFFERING OF THE PIPE

CONTENT

1. Smoking the pipe is a device the storyteller uses to invoke the powers which act as his muse, to extend friendship, and to create a common bond with his audience. He concludes the narrative saying, "Now, my friend, let us smoke together so that there may be only good between us."

2. The ribbons represent the four quarters of the universe (north, south, east, and west) and the four seasons.

3. The young woman is a supernatural being who comes to Black Elk's people to give them the pipe of peace and prosperity.

4. Black Elk prays to the "great spirit," whom he calls *grandfather.* He prays in part to stimulate his own memory and in part to indicate his reverence for the "one" who has seen everything since the beginning of time.

STRATEGIES AND STRUCTURES

1. Black Elk digresses from his main narrative—the story of his life as a holy man of the Oglala Sioux—to tell the story about the origins of the pipe which the buffalo woman brings to the chief.

2. The author explains the origins of the pipe through a narrative/ storytelling. The story itself takes on mythic dimensions, enhancing the cultural and historical significance of the pipe.

3. The ceremony at the beginning and end of the story acts as a framing device for the entire tale. It creates boundaries for the story and unifies it.

ALICE WALKER

JOURNEY TO NINE MILES

CONTENT

1. Walker was participating in political causes, writing her own books, and indulging in more local than worldly activities. She was listening to music like that of B. B. King and the Beatles. She became aware of Bob Marley's music when spending time with some friends while writing the screenplay for *The Color Purple.*

2. Her love of Marley leads her on a pilgrimage to "Nine Miles," Marley's grave in Jamaica. She finds small, simple farms inhabited by poor people.

3. Rather than finding the "attentiveness and joy" of the Rasta culture that she expects to, Walker learns that while Jamaican people are friendly and humble, these also are very poor.

4. America sells "Elvis Presley," "James Dean," and "Marilyn Monroe," as it tries to profit from the nostalgia and sentimentality created by such figures.

STRATEGIES AND STRUCTURES

1. Walker uses a journey motif because she is discovering herself as she makes a spiritual journey toward a more sophisticated understanding of Rasta.

2. The author employs transitional devices that indicate time order, beginning when she first heard Bob Marley to when she finished her script and ultimately took a trip to Jamaica. In Jamaica we follow her as she and her family travel to "Nine Miles."

3. Walker contrasts images of joy and hardship during the first part of her essay (i.e., several images of dancing are contrasted with images of the poverty of Jamaica).

4. She converts from an angry tourist who must change her tire three times before even arriving at her destination to one who feels at peace with the Rasta culture and learns that "There is no poverty, only richness in this."

LOUISE ERDRICH

AMERICAN HORSE

CONTENT

1. The bulk of Erdrich's narrative focuses on two parent/child relationships. Two things are happening. *In the present,* three people— Vickie Koob, Officer Brackett, and Harmony—have come to take Buddy away from Albertine and her life-style. In doing so, there is a self-righteous assumption that Buddy will receive more than he will lose by separating him from his mother. What could someone who "seems" to have no socially redeemable qualities offer a child? Buddy's natural inclination to thank Koob for the chocolate bar "as his mother had taught him" and the incident with the dead butterfly, Albertine and American Horse suggest that nurturing and/or growth occurred between parent and child—regardless of how things "seemed" to others. *In the past,* American Horse transferred a sense of strength into Albertine—something that had endured to the day Buddy was taken away from her. The link between parental love in the past and present—however imperfect—is expressed in paragraph 80. In a desperate attempt to keep Harmony and the others from Buddy, Albertine rushed Harmony and "on wings of her father's hands, on dead butterfly wings, Albertine lifted into the air and flew toward the others. . . . It was her father throwing her up into the air and out of danger. Her arms opened wide for bullets but no bullets came. Harmony did not shoot."

2. Harmony wants the State Patrol to realize that he was "a tribal police officer who could be counted on" to help them—someone who did not favor Indians, regardless of his ethnic background.

3. American Horse was Albertine's father and, therefore, Buddy's grandfather. Responses regarding his significance in this narrative will vary.

4. Albertine felt spiritually uplifted. She felt the wisdom and the "grace" of the butterfly and also "felt the same kind of possibilities and closed her eyes almost in shock or pain, she felt so light and powerful at that moment."

5. As she is being driven away from his family—his life as he knows it—Buddy realizes that he has been separated from his mother, a person who loves and cares for him. Now he is alone.

STRATEGIES AND STRUCTURES

1. The four distinct parts of Erdrich's narrative include: 1) Buddy's observation of Albertine while she sleeps and Vickie Koob, Officer

Brackett, and Harmony approach (paragraphs 1-9); 2) the interaction between Lawrence and the three "would be" liberators (paragraph 20-64); 3) the flashback to Albertine's childhood and the incident with American Horse and the dead butterfly and the confrontation between Harmony and Albertine in the present (paragraphs 64-81); 4) Harmony, Vickie Koob, and Officer Brackett driving away from the scene (paragraphs 82-85).

2. The transitions and linking words help the narrative to move from one point to the next coherently and effectively. Since parts of this story move from the present to the past back to the present again, clear time transitions are essential to keep the chronology of events straight.

3. The narrative begins and concludes with Buddy engaged in the action, thereby framing the short story. The story begins with Buddy looking at Albertine, his mother, as she slept, and Vickie Koob, Officer Brackett, and Harmony approach the house to claim custody of him. The story concludes as he is being driven away from his home. At that time, Buddy again is looking at his mother—this time through a car window—and he begins to scream when he realizes what has actually occurred: his roots have been left behind him and so has his mother.

4. At one point in the story, every character observes some idiosyncrasy of another. This achieves two things: 1) we become aware of details pertaining to individual characters, 2) we learn something about the observers. A good scene to point to as an example of this would be when Officer Brackett tries to take a look at Vickie Koob's copious notes and they fight playfully over them. She writes, "Officer Brackett displays an undue amount of interest in my work."

NGUYEN NGOC NGAN
SAIGON, APRIL 1975

CONTENT

1. The author describes the horror of the American evacuation of Saigon at the end of the Vietnam War. The unavoidable conflict he faces is having to leave his homeland and then trying to get out. He must do this or be taken prisoner by the Viet Cong.

2. Ngan is angry with the BBC because the network is constantly making announcements of the fall of cities to the north before it happens. Because his anger is brought on by his fear, it is understandable but not necessarily justified because the BBC does correctly predict that the Viet Cong will take over Saigon tomorrow.

3. The author's world, in which he had enjoyed freedom in warfare, ended because the North Vietnamese Army was taking over South Vietnam. As a result he is forced to destroy all records of his previous life to avoid being taken prisoner.

STRATEGIES AND STRUCTURES

1. The author strengthens his narrative because he can give so many specific examples taken from his own experiences.

2. The tone or mood is a foreboding sense of doom mixed with terror. His early descriptions of the bombardment of the city and his wife's refusal to leave her mother, her memories of "the Hue horror of Tet, 1968," and his inability to get any transportation out of Vietnam foreshadow his impending sense of doom.

3. Answers will vary.

4. Details which suggest sadness, horror, and doom make his descriptions vivid and clear (e.g., the images of his burning everything from his past that would connect him with the fallen regime, the images of weapons, and the images of so many people on the beach with only a few boats in which to escape).

Description

APPROACHES TO DESCRIPTION

1. To show readers precisely what descriptive words can do in further-ing the sense of an essay, attempt to assist them in building a critical ear in the following manner: Walk into class and turn to one of the essays in the Description Chapter. Begin class by reading a few pas-sages, particularly accentuating words that describe—words which show how or why something is happening. Stop. Then have a stu-dent pick up where you left off reading in the same manner that you did, accentuating descriptive words as they come to them. (It may help to tell your students that it is beneficial in life to be a ham. That way they won't feel peculiar about pronouncing descriptive words loudly and clearly.)

2. Figurative language oftentimes eludes the basic writer, but it is en-joyable and is within everyone's grasp with a little guidance. On the blackboard write the beginning of several similes (e.g., large as a _____, lonely as a _____, dirty as a _____, and as sad as _____). Have your students complete these similes by giv-ing you an image of an animal, object, or a plant that is most appro-priate. You may want to give a few of your own images as models. You might try the same process with metaphors.

TOSHIO MORI

The Woman Who Made Swell Doughnuts

CONTENT

1. Responses will vary to this question.

2. Mori respects the woman who makes swell doughnuts because she has lived a hard life and yet has maintained a giving and caring attitude.

3. The author writes about her before her death because "it would be a shame to talk of her doughnuts after she is dead, after she is formless."

4. The doughnuts, like the woman, are simple and plain and yet "different, unique."

STRATEGIES AND STRUCTURES

1. The controlling metaphor of the circle in paragraph 6 suggests that the woman is a small circle, keeping her life within its boundaries. The controlling image of silence in paragraph 10 suggests that even when words are not spoken, communication is constant through a nod of the head. In a world of noise and confusion, her world is quiet and serene.

2. In paragraph 2, Mori gives specific examples from the woman's life, each indicating a different role she has played: mother, field worker, housewife, and grandmother.

3. Mori uses dialogue to highlight this special relationship between the old woman and him. The overuse of dialogue would diminish its effect.

4. The author gives specific examples of the type of experiences the elderly woman has lived through (e.g., giving birth to six children, working in fields, and working around the house) to suggest she has had varied experiences in her life. Moreover, he also says she has faced "the summers and winters and also the springs and autumns" to infer that she has lived a long time.

MAYA ANGELOU

CHAMPION OF THE WORLD

CONTENT

1. Everyone was gathered in Uncle Willie's store to listen to the radio broadcast of a Joe Louis (the Brown Bomber) fight. Even the "old Christian ladies" were there anticipating Joe Louis's victory over his contender.

2. Due to the racism that pervaded this southern town, people who lived some distance from the store made arrangements to stay in town overnight to avoid any entanglements with individuals who might be angry about a Joe Louis win and, thus, would take out their aggressiveness on the nearest African-American.

3. Besides defending his heavyweight crown, Joe Louis is also figuratively upholding the pride and dignity of the African-American. His win was symbolic in that it proved to the world that African-Americans are just as capable of being on top as any other individual. As Angelou put it, ". . . Joe Louis had proved that we were the strongest people in the world."

4. Those who were in Uncle Willie's store were captivated by every word the radio announcer said (e.g. "It's another to the body, and it looks like Joe Louis is going down." The listeners were devastated by the news: "We didn't breathe. We didn't hope. We waited.").

5. Everyone would celebrate in his or her own way. The Christian ladies would buy soft drinks, and "Some of the men went behind the Store and poured white lightning into their soft-drink bottles, and a few of the bigger boys followed them."

STRATEGIES AND STRUCTURES

1. The major function of dialogue in "Champion of the World" is to retell the story through the eyes of the radio announcer. As the information imparted by the announcer provides the basis for the tension in this story, a great deal would have been lost if it had been omitted. Indeed, if there had been no Joe Louis fight broadcast over the radio, there would have been no reason for people to gather at Uncle Willie's store that night.

2. Short, periodic sentences tend to heighten suspense in this narrative. We know the narrator feels the same as the other people in the store because, like everyone else, she is delighted that Joe Louis has won, for he has defended more than just his heavyweight title.

3. Details from this story will vary from student to student.

4. First of all, there was not an "inch of space" left in Uncle Willie's store for people to stand and listen to the boxing match. As people often do when they're nervous or apprehensive, there are short spurts of dialogue, such as, "I ain't worried 'bout this fight. Joe's gonna whip that cracker like it's open season."

RUSSELL C. LEONG

NOTES FROM A SON TO HIS FATHER

CONTENT

1. This question calls for a value judgment on the part of the student, which should be supported with specific examples from the text of the essay.

2. Leong feels frustrated when he attempts to describe his father because of the small amount of information he has about him. He goes on to say, ". . . I feel like a small child pressing a string of hard beads to my chest, a rosary of sorts, chanting the same phrases and images a thousand times in order to derive an order, a strength out of them. But the polished beads do not yield a thing: it is a repetition of uselessness."

3. Leong first sees his father as a man who spends a great amount of time sharpening his cleaver in order to chop the vegetables and fruits that he has arranged on the table. In contrast to the industrious cook is the image of his father "glittering in anger, a knife poised in his hand, his face is pulsing pink, the once pale cauliflower flesh tinged with color and rage, and he is on one side of the room about to throw the knife into me."

4. Leong contends that a son ". . . must realize his peculiar tendency to be, i.e., manly and so he searches." He admits that he accomplished this by going out on the streets to look for the ". . . peculiar stuff of which pictures, pride, and parades are made of."

STRATEGIES AND STRUCTURES

1. Leong's opening paragraphs reveal the gap between him and his father. He is not happy about his position, as indicated by the opening sentence, "There is nothing good about being a son; I know; I am a son."

2. In the third paragraph, the author's images appeal especially to a person's sight, sound, and taste. In particular, the author refers to the sight of fresh fruits and vegetables, the sound of "Zhap zhap zhap" as his father sharpens his cleaver, and the taste of items like "the jade bitter melon."

3. There are many images that go into the vivid description of Leong's bedroom in paragraph 7. While the author is cringing in fear, his father is pulsating in anger, making threats that he never will carry out. The father has ". . . inherited bitterness from some vague source, from a life not his own, a frustration that has finally found its

point in a knife, a silver gleaming tooth that will draw blood from my chest."

4. The distance between the father and son is always being emphasized in this essay, creating a unifying theme. The author mentions a number of times how he wanted to be with his father; indeed, he said that "as a child I dreamed of my father."

5. Just as the theme of disillusionment runs throughout the essay (dreams or wishes versus confrontation with reality), the essay concludes with the author once more searching for an ideal and finding himself unfulfilled as he finds himself in the middle of the dilemma of the love between a father and a son.

KATHERINE BARRETT
OLD BEFORE HER TIME

CONTENT

1. Barrett's essay traces how Patty Moore explored ". . . the culture of youth and beauty when your hair is gray, your skin is wrinkled, and no men turn their heads as you pass," by dressing up as an elderly woman. In doing so, Barrett shows how Moore encountered prejudice and indignities wherever she went.

2. She impersonated an elderly citizen over 200 times in 14 states.

3. Moore's reasons for charading as a senior citizen were highly personal. When she began her project in 1979, her own "life seemed to be falling apart" because of the recent failure of her marriage.

4. Moore's exposure to the abysmal treatment of elderly people, coupled with her observation of how they "pick themselves up after something bad—or even something catastrophic—happened," strengthened her as a human being. She found that seeing the extremes that the elderly had to confront on a daily basis enabled her to recover from the trauma in her own life.

STRATEGIES AND STRUCTURES

1. The seven lessons concerning elderly people that Patty Moore learned are as follows: (1) "The old are often ignored"; (2) "The fear of crime is paralyzing"; (3) "If small, thoughtless deficiencies in design were corrected, life would be so much easier for older people"; (4) "Even a fifty-year-old marriage isn't necessarily a good one"; (5) "Social class affects every aspect of an older person's existence"; (6) "You never grow old emotionally. You always need to feel loved";

and (7) "Life does go on. . . as long as you're flexible and open to change." The aforementioned seven lessons were all steps leading to her ultimate perception of elderly people: "Their bodies age but inside they are no different than when they were young."

2. Since all the words in boldfaced type indicate cities and dates, the reader knows that Patty is on the move, trying to ascertain if the treatment of elderly people is the same throughout the United States.

3. Answers will vary to this question.

4. Barrett integrates short anecdotes with dialogues to keep her reader's attention. A sense of momentum builds with each new experience, topped off by stating a specific lesson that Moore has learned.

N. SCOTT MOMADAY

FROM *THE WAY TO RAINY MOUNTAIN*

CONTENT

1. Momaday returns to Rainy Mountain to be at his grandmother's grave. His trip causes him to reflect on both the history of his people, the Kiowas, and his grandmother's life in particular.

2. Momaday's grandmother is the central character of this essay. Like her ancestors, the grandmother, Aho, had a reverence for the sun and spent much of her time praying. She also was a teller of stories (most of Momaday's knowledge of the legends came from her) and she loved to cook and entertain when she was young. He was told that in the face of death, she was childlike.

3. The Kiowas were a mountain people who nearly 300 years ago came to Oklahoma from Montana, and on the way the Crows taught them the ways of the Plains, so that by the time they arrived at their destination they had been transformed. "No longer were they slaves to the simple necessity of survival; they were a lordly and dangerous society of fighters and thieves, hunters and priests of the sun." It would seem that the harsh environment around Rainy Mountain was where the Kiowas were driven by the U.S. government. Though not directly stated, this area undoubtedly is a reservation. (The badlands of Oklahoma became the final depository for many Indian tribes in the late 1800s.)

4. Aside from the journey home to visit his grandmother's grave, Momaday takes a mental journey through the ages tracing the history of his people and the life of his grandmother. After spending the majority of the essay on a nonphysical journey, he concludes by actually visiting the grave of his grandmother.

STRATEGIES AND STRUCTURES

1. The primary mood of Momaday's opening description is somber. He accomplishes this by his vivid description of a harsh, desolate landscape. Not without its beauty, there is an attraction to this land which makes one ". . . lose the sense of proportion [while] . . . imagination comes to life . . ." At the completion of this description, Momaday states, ". . . this, you think, is where Creation was begun," which leads to an introspective look at his past.

2. Both the Kiowas and his grandmother have had to endure hardships and suffering as well as having to adapt to new surroundings and cultures.

3. Momaday can recall his grandmother only in his memory, but he does so vividly. For instance, he sees her standing at the stove, sitting by the window, and bending over her beadwork. He hears her uttering long, rambling prayers. Momaday's reference to her cooking could also elicit a reader response to other senses such as taste and smell.

4. There are two distinct differences in the descriptions of his grandmother's house. Originally the house was full of visitors, feasting, life, and vitality; however, by the time he reaches paragraph 16, Momaday describes the same structure by saying, "Now there is funeral silence in the rooms. . . . The walls have closed in upon my grandmother's house."

5. In the final paragraph there is a distinct change in mood. The author has completed his nostalgic mental journey, and after visiting the grave of his grandmother, he takes one last look at the mountain and continues on with his life.

BARBARA GRAHAM

CONFESSIONS OF A QUIT ADDICT

CONTENT

1. When the author finally heard Leary speak, she had already quit college; therefore, she in some way was ahead of him. She is a good candidate for his "battle cry" because she had always had difficulty following through with difficulties she had begun. In her own words, "Even when I was a young girl, it was obvious that I had been born without the stick-to-it, nose-to-the-grindstone gene." In fact, she speaks of quitting in terms of a "rush," that is an "instant high of cutting loose."

2. Her husband, Brian, was her perfect collaborator in the art of quitting. She became his loyal apprentice when they sold all their possessions, quit their jobs, and "fled to Europe." Soon a distinct pattern developed: they would live in one place, dream of another, work at odd jobs (she notes her odd jobs as including "secretary, sales clerk, cocktail waitress, draft counselor, nude model, warehouse clerk, candlemaker"), and they would earn "just enough money to get [them] to the next destination." No matter where they went, however, whether it was British Columbia, California, or Colorado, they never were satisfied.

3. One of Graham's last schemes to find "true happiness," and to get close to nature was to build her own house in Northern California. However, when this plan "fell apart," she simply "snapped." At that moment, she realized that she was unable to live on fantasies of what could or will be. Since private demons "followed them wherever they went." Graham discovered that she and her husband could "shed their surroundings" but not escape their "own skin." Ironically she traveled thousands of miles and had one child before she understood that the "quitting [I] took for freedom was as much of a trap as the social conventions we were trying to escape." More than anything Graham realized that she wanted to "land somewhere," to belong.

4. The negativity associated with any "recovering addict" is one reason she does not identify herself as one. After all, in many respects, she considers her past act of quitting—regardless of what she thinks now—as often "the best, most honest, and most creative response to a life situation." Since leaving the father of her son, Graham has been a publicist, gone to college a second time (and dropped out again), as well as moved across the country twice. Presently she is a writer.

5. The author now finds her life to be more "interesting, more richly satisfying" and she believes she never would have become close to her family nor developed good friends if she had not settled down. She further notes that, "no matter how hard we try to be the sole authors of our own stories, life eventually will have its way and quit us."

STRATEGIES AND STRUCTURES

1. By beginning her essay with Timothy Leary's chant, "Turn on, tune in, drop out," Graham establishes the historical context of her journeys as a quit artist. In 1967, there was a clear counterculture movement, a movement which questioned the status quo of society as well as some of the ideologies some people had taken for granted (e.g., it is a privilege to be a member of the armed forces and fight out country's battles whether they are justified or not). The summer of 1967 was also titled "The Summer of Love," and many people

embraced the notion of sex, love, and rock and roll, things which mainstream society criticized as escapism. Graham's essay points out to the reader that quitting was looked down on by society, but she would appear as a heroine to her peers.

2. Metaphorically speaking, Graham divides her essay into two parts of a journey. The first part talks about the social climate at the time that made it perfectly acceptable or even desirable to quit and turn one's back on society. The 1960s were a time when social inequality and racism were brought to everyone's attention. Thus, by refusing to buy into the established social norm, Graham and her husband were essentially looking for fulfillment in another place with other people and different attitudes. Maybe they were looking for something better, but the author finally realized that the problem was within herself, and this brings about the second half of the journey: settling down. It was with this enlightenment that she knew she had to settle down and make a home for her son, thus, producing the second part of her journey. How and why she found satisfaction in becoming rooted in a place, in an occupation, and in a relationship concludes her journey.

3. Graham does not consider herself a "recovering quitter" because she still has the impulse within herself to quit. To recover suggests that the feeling to quit, or that gene she blames for making her quit, would be cured or would leave her. She doesn't want us to jump to any conclusions because regardless of the fact that she has quit so many occupations and relationships, the ability to quit is the driving force behind her uniqueness. She would not want to be labeled as a "recovering quitter" or conventional person any more than she would want to be stereotyped as a quit artist.

4. She begins the essay by telling us that she is a quitter, quite possibly to allow us to establish expectations as to where she is going in her essay. The very title of her essay, "Confessions of a Quit Addict," suggests that she is atoning for her past transgressions in life by offering readers a testimonial. This, however, is not the case. True, she comes to realize that escaping the conventional world by moving from one place to another merely entraps her as much as the society she is fleeing from, but if she were to give up her idealism about the power of quitting, it would make her another faceless being in the crowd. In part, we are delighted that she does not proclaim that she has totally recovered or has healed. This would have made the essay just another predictable confession. Instead, she surprises us.

Illustration and Example

APPROACHES TO ILLUSTRATION AND EXAMPLE

1. A good way to introduce illustration is to have students define abstract terms by using folk tales of their own culture or ones they know something about. Have them give you examples of people who are evil, generous, heroic, and greedy, and have them explain why they chose such a person, as well as give details to support their choices.

2. Give the students a list of abstract terms, such as "beautiful," "handsome," "poor," "wealthy." Then have the students go through different magazines searching for "illustrations" of these terms. Finally, have them explain in a journal entry why they chose the pictures that they did. Explain to them that their pictures illustrate vague concepts with specific details and images.

NIKKI GIOVANNI

MY OWN STYLE

CONTENT

1. Giovanni notes that younger women are proud of their inability to do certain things, as if that makes them modern. She congratulates them on their internationalism. While we can definitely state that the tone of this essay is somewhat ironic, interpretations to the third part of this question may have a variety of answers.

2. She differs from other women in that she is not as artificial since she wears no makeup. She is much more practical because she collects useful articles like soaps and candles.

3. The author feels that the African American community, though 40 percent unemployed at the time this was written, will improve its economic standing in society by the upward movement of the BUMP.

STRATEGIES AND STRUCTURES

1. Giovanni devotes the first few paragraphs comparing herself to other women in order to establish that she is proud of herself, pointing out how different she is, and at the same time, establishes the theme of the essay.

2. The author uses several examples to show that she never has sacrificed her individual style, i.e., she can cook a gourmet dinner in 15 minutes and is not afraid to quote the old folks to support her claims.

3. The author uses a tongue-in-cheek tone to establish her ultimate purpose, which is to mock uniformity.

JACK KROLL
Roll Over Bach, Too

CONTENT

1. The controlling idea of this essay revolves around how the Beatles became the epitome of pop culture. Kroll notes that "what linked the screechers and the scholars was a sense of something new, an absolute freshness that the Beatles manifested musically and personally." Combined, these qualities formed the nucleus for a "creative surge," a surge that had been absent for a long time in popular music.

2. In paragraph 4, Kroll specifically mentions Chuck Berry and Little Richard as pioneer rockers. You might point out that Chuck Berry wrote "Roll Over Beethoven" in the mid-50s, at the onslaught of rock and roll. You might also have your students refer to the Pre-reading Question number 2, to point out why Kroll called his essay "Roll Over Bach, Too."

3. By referring to people like Charlie Chaplin, Buster Keaton (renowned silent film actors), and Louis Armstrong, and Duke

Ellington (influential jazz musicians)—individuals who defied being categorized and remembered for a brief moment in time— Kroll is able to demonstrate how the Beatles, too, "made it clear that if art is to survive in the techno-millennium that looms ahead, it must be hooked into the reality and redemptions in the days of our lives."

4. Answers will vary; however, you might wish to use this question as an essay topic in its own right.

5. Kroll suggests that "the Beatles, like 'other geniuses such as Bach, Mozart, and Beethoven, knew the right time and place to be born.'" To be sure, all the classical composers and the Beatles were extremely talented, yet it was a matter of time and place that enabled all of them to showcase their abilities to their best advantage.

STRATEGIES AND STRUCTURES

1. Kroll gives many examples of the Beatles' popularity, beginning with "eeeeeeeeeeeeeeeee . . ." and then he progresses by listing their most popular songs and concludes with illustrations and examples which demonstrate why albums such as "Sgt. Pepper" mark "an epochal event, the matriculation of rock into high art."

2. Kroll begins his essay with the rhetorical question, "Were you there?" The answer to this question, of course, leads into the controlling idea of the essay, which is the Beatles broke through the musical doldrums of the early 1960s and left behind "the most thrilling creative surge of popular music" in the latter half of the twentieth century.

3. Kroll's purpose in comparing "A Day in the Life" with T. S. Eliot's apocalyptic poem, "The Waste Land," is to demonstrate that the Beatles' lyrics are no less impressive and thought-provoking than those of Eliot, a learned and respected scholar.

4. By presenting viewpoints from other critics of the Beatles, the author shows his readers that what he claims is not an isolated perception. That is, many individuals have felt the power and influence which resulted from the works of the Beatles. You may want to use this question to examine the value of diverse testimonies as supporting material. Answers will vary for the latter part of this question.

5. Answers will vary here; however, if the author were unable to refer to specific songs, readers would doubt or not be influenced by what he claims.

PHILIP K. CHIU

THE MYTH OF THE MODEL MINORITY

CONTENT

1. The Chinese Americans were labeled "The Model Minority" because all reports indicated that they were law-abiding citizens who performed well academically. The news media were responsible for perpetuating these myths.

2. The stereotypes they have had to endure are those of "the insidious Fu Manchu," the "inscrutable Charlie Chan," the ruthless invaders of the Korean War, and "slant-eyed, ever obedient little men toiling about with their pigtails freshly cut off."

3. He wants us to know that while some are super achievers, most Chinese Americans are normal human beings.

4. Chiu requests that the media portray Chinese Americans as they really are.

STRATEGIES AND STRUCTURES

1. Chiu begins his essay by referring to the media, showing how the Chinese Americans have been stereotyped as a society. By concluding the essay with a similar reference to the news media, he comes full-circle, creating a sense of closure.

2. By drawing on common and popular cultural references, such as Fu Manchu and Charlie Chan, Chiu assures us that most of his readers will be familiar with the stereotypes he is criticizing. In the concluding paragraph, Chiu demonstrates that the average Chinese American is often "unremarkable" and can be found in neither extreme.

3. Obviously, the media have simplified the complexity of the Chinese American (human) character, and Chiu's history illustrates this. Student responses to what Chiu asserts are motivating factors behind a crime are bound to vary. Generally speaking though, the crimes Chiu mentions are less important to him than the point that Chinese Americans are *no longer* model citizens; they are human beings who get involved in any number of depraved activities. (To approach this same question from a different angle, you might want to ask your students if Chiu *seems* to rationalize some of the crimes he lists in paragraph 10.)

BARBARA MIKULSKI

A POLISH AMERICAN SPEAKS UP: THE MYTH OF THE MELTING POT

CONTENT

1. The Melting Pot theory is invalid, for rather than peoples' races, cultures, and traditions blending together and working as one, groups in society are separated because of prejudices, fears, and viewpoints. She feels that we need an alliance of workers.

2. Governments at all levels overtax and underserve the ethnic Americans.

3. The specific problems faced by ethnic Americans include: restrictive eligibility requirements to buy a home, i.e., an ethnic American often can't get an FHA loan and is forced to live in poorer neighborhoods, his/her income oftentimes is low, and he or she is the first to be laid off.

4. The ethnic American feels looked down upon because he or she is treated as a product rather than a human being.

STRATEGIES AND STRUCTURES

1. Mikulski's two opening sentences set the tone for the essay by taking a firm, argumentative stance against the notion of a melting pot.

2. Each paragraph has one controlling idea. Paragraph 2 discusses the government's inadequacies, paragraph 3 discusses the economic injustices, and paragraph 4 explores the social indifference.

3. The author makes specific references to the problems of the elderly, the blue-collar worker, the first-time homeowner to illustrate the government's failure to assist ethnic Americans.

4. Mikulski does not merely summarize her main points; she offers a recommendation that ethnic Americans should band together to form political organizations of their own.

STEPHANIE ERICSSON

THE WAYS WE LIE

CONTENT

1. Ericsson categorizes the lies as: white lies, façades, deflecting, omission, stereotypes and clichés, groupthink, out-and-out lies, dismissal, and delusion.

2. According to the author, "The white lie assumes that the truth will cause more damage than a simple, harmless untruth." In other words, if you compliment people on their appearance when in reality they look "like hell," you are doing them a greater disservice than if you had been honest. She does mention, however, that not all situations are "cut-and-dried."

3. Façades are destructive because they seduce others into illusion, into accepting a false front without analyzing someone's past further.

4. Ericsson likes the "out-and-out lies" the best because she says she can trust the "bald-faced lie." She knows where she stands with such lies, for they don't toy with her perceptions: rather, they argue with them. Finally, she says, "If this were the only form of lying there would be no such thing as floating anxiety or the adult-children of alcoholics movement.

5. Ericsson defines delusion as: "a cousin of dismissal . . . the tendency to see excuses as facts. It's a powerful lying tool because it filters out information that contradicts what we want to believe."

STRATEGIES AND STRUCTURES

1. First and foremost, the anecdote stimulates the reader's interest in the topic as well as sets the theme of the essay.

2. Her topic sentences frequently define the lie she is discussing. With a clear frame of reference, her ensuing explanation and analysis of a lie make sense. To illustrate the different categories of lies, Ericsson provides examples from her personal experiences, observations, and readings.

3. This essay has a clear introduction, body, and conclusion. The introduction sets the theme and leads to her presentation of the various kinds of lies. Her analyses of the various lies comprise the body of the essay. In her concluding paragraphs she admits that she has mentioned only "a few of the ways we lie. Or are lied to." Nonetheless, she asks us to reevaluate our positions on lying and to consider what harm is caused by lying.

4. Answers will vary in respect to the rhetorical questions.

Definition

APPROACHES TO DEFINITION

1. Open class by asking students what types of movies they like to watch (e.g., westerns, science fiction, adventure films, etc.). Write each on the board, requesting *what* the genre in question contains (e.g., what elements does a western typically contain?). Then have everyone jot down a brief explanation—a definition written for someone who has never heard of the term—for each genre in his/her notebook or journal. Finally, move into a general discussion of how definition functions in expository writing.

2. Give a short mini-lesson on the origins of several racist terms, and show how these words attack or degrade specific qualities of an ethnic group. By giving the historical definition of the word, you can show your students how racism evolves and/or perpetuates itself.

ISAAC ASIMOV
WHAT IS INTELLIGENCE, ANYWAY?

CONTENT

1. According to Asimov, intelligence is the knowledge and ability to perform specific tasks well in any given vocation. That is, intelligence is not limited to I.Q. tests and academic learning.

2. Asimov has the type of intelligence that is good for answering academic questions. Such intelligence is beneficial when taking I.Q. tests but is of limited use when fixing one's car or performing other manual labor.

3. Initially, Asimov felt that because he always scored high on I.Q. tests, he was highly intelligent, and he expected "other people to think so, too." He reconsiders his position on intelligence after his visit to the auto repair man, an individual who "could not possibly have scored more than 80" on an I.Q. test, and yet was a wizard when it came to locating and fixing problems with Asimov's car, a task Asimov—with all his scholastic knowledge—was incapable of doing.

STRATEGIES AND STRUCTURES

1. The numerous episodes in this essay help Asimov to demonstrate many different types of intelligence. Basically, Asimov builds his definition of intelligence by example.

2. Since Asimov's ultimate point is to question the socially accepted notion of intelligence, it is useful to present the popular definition of intelligence before setting out to show why such a definition is unsatisfactory.

3. The single sentence paragraph emphasizes his conclusion that intelligence has more to do with the practical application of one's knowledge than scholastic abilities.

JO GOODWIN PARKER

WHAT IS POVERTY?

CONTENT

1. Parker claims poverty is living in a "smell" (paragraph 2), being tired (paragraph 3), living in dirt (paragraph 4), having few resources (paragraph 5), seeking assistance (paragraphs 6 and 7), having sad, painful memories (paragraphs 8 and 9), despairing about the present and future (paragraphs 10, 11, 12), and losing pride (paragraph 13).

2. Parker tends to talk about her children and the problems they face throughout the essay. Some of the difficulties they faced when growing up included poor nutrition and health care, inadequate clothing, and crime-filled neighborhoods.

3. Though Parker attempts to get assistance from social programs and health clinics, the help she actually receives is frequently inadequate (she receives only $78.00 a month to support three children) or too difficult to obtain (e.g., the health clinic is in town, eight miles from where she lives).

4. People often feel help is available through social programs, but they do not realize the difficulties the poor have in obtaining the much-needed assistance. As a result, such people remain ignorant about the poor and their ability to acquire many necessities of life, and, therefore, do not assist Parker or other individuals living at the poverty level.

STRATEGIES AND STRUCTURES

1. Parker uses a traditional topic sentence to begin most of her paragraphs. Most of these topic sentences begin with, "Poverty is . . . ," creating a haunting repetition.

2. Parker develops each paragraph through the use of specific examples drawn from her personal experiences and observations. The memorable details in this essay will vary from student to student.

3. As mentioned previously, Parker found the usual solutions "society has for poverty" inadequate or difficult to obtain. Parker concludes her essay with a rhetorical question ("Can you be silent too?") in order to get the reader to reflect on his/her current attitudes about the poor and what they need to survive and to motivate him/her to take action against poverty.

GUILLERMO GÓMEZ-PEÑA
DOCUMENTED/UNDOCUMENTED

CONTENT

1. By using words such as "fissure," "fractured," and "wound," Gómez-Peña immediately begins his essay with images of division and splintering. He is caught between two societies, two ways of living, and, as a result, he seems disoriented—a man with a fractured sense of reality.

2. The "chilangos" originally came from Mexico City to North America, attempting to escape social and ecological problems.

3. Many people call Gómez-Peña several names: chilango, mexiquillo, pocho, norteño, sudacca, Hispanic, and Latino. He calls himself Mexican, Chicano, and Latin American.

4. Because Gómez-Peña is caught between two worlds and feels as if he is not part of either, he must constantly redefine himself to sustain a sense of identity. Ultimately, traveling between both worlds and researching his past allows him to maintain the two sides of his identities.

STRATEGIES AND STRUCTURES

1. The opening sentence introduces the theme of "division" by giving the reader images such as "fissure" and "border." Immediately the reader feels the tension of a man with a divided identity and realizes the essay will explore the difficult position of living between two worlds, with no definite place in either.

2. Gómez-Peña defines himself by explaining the historical origins of his people and by contrasting his definition of himself to the way others define him. Each method he uses for defining himself becomes a major part of the essay.

3. Gómez-Peña has documented who he feels he is and has come to realize that he has not really been documented (acknowledged) in either culture. Bearing this in mind, the title suggests the two parts of his implied thesis.

JANE AND MICHAEL STERN

VALLEY GIRLS

CONTENT

1. The final sentence in paragraph one, "In the summer of 1982, the San Fernando Valley had a moment in the sun," sets the stage for the entire essay. In 1982, Jodie Ann Posserello, in collaboration with Sue Blank, wrote *The Totally Awesome Val Guide. . . .* Jane and Michael Stern follow the genesis of the "Valley Girl"—from adolescent girls cruising malls in the San Fernando Valley to the "Valley Girl" archetype who could be spotted at malls in every corner of the United States.

2. Moon Unit Zappa, the daughter of musician/composer Frank Zappa, had listened to the *Val-speak* jargon and noted the behavior of her friends and imitated them at home. Amused, her father took Moon Unit to a studio where they made a record called "Valley Girl." The record featured—and satirized—language that became known as *Val-speak,* language that often managed to make statements seem like questions.

3. A Val would most likely be a middle-class, adolescent girl who loves to shop for clothes, spends time preening her nails and hair, and in general, attempts to impress her peers. Additionally, a *Val* spoke jargon and had a "stick your tongue out and wiggle" attitude. According to Moon Unit Zappa, one could find a *Val* in almost any shopping mall in the United States in 1992.

4. *Val-speak,* much of which was originally surfer jargon (e.g., *tubular* in surfer jargon meant "great wave"; in "*Val-speak,*" *tubular* refers to anything *excellent*), gave society the first group to offer new *pop vocabulary* since the middle of the seventies when the trucker/CB radio craze captured the people's fancy with such words (jargon) and phrases as: "smokey" (a police or highway patrol officer), "let the hammer down" (to speed), "ten-four" (message received), "eight-seven" (the place sucks), and so on. Furthermore, the blasé, egotistical rudeness of *Val-speak* offered an *attitude* to match its "zesty vocabulary." You might suggest that your students locate a copy of *The Totally Awesome Val Guide . . .* by Jodie Ann Posserello—as told to Sue Black—for an in-depth catalogue of *Val-speak* terms. As a follow-up activity to the second *Language and Vocabulary* question, you might have students locate and research information in *The Totally Awesome Val Guide. . . .*

5. Three years after the heyday of the Valley Girl summer, 1982, *Newsweek* magazine pointed out that the fashionable appearance of the "total Val" had changed: "Ruffled blouses, miniskirts, costume jewelry, and shaggy hair had become totally uncool." The old models for Valley girls such as Jamie Lee Curtis and Brooke Shields had become *passé* because they had matured too much and no longer personified the ideal traits of middle-class "insolent materialism." In their place, the lasting manifestation of the *Valley Girl* style is epitomized—or eternalized, if you will—by Madonna.

STRATEGIES AND STRUCTURES

1. Definition is used in many ways throughout "Valley Girls." On one hand, the authors develop their essay by defining the history of the term *Valley girl* (*valley* originally referred to San Fernando Valley where "there are malls, and in those malls rove adolescent girls"; the latter half of the term, *girls* is self-explanatory). They go on to discuss how Moon Unit Zappa helped popularize *Val-speak,* and conclude their essay mentioning the transformed state of the vacuous, material *Valley Girl.* "Definition by Example" is also used to develop this essay. In paragraph four, for instance, the authors cite examples of what they consider some "essential Val-speak terms, as catalogued by *The Totally Awesome Val Guide . . . .*" along with a definition of each "essential" term (e.g., *bitchen* means "the best thing you can say about something"; *fer sure* is defined as the "first words a Valley baby learns to speak"; *like* is "the hamburger helper of Valley conversation. It goes hand-in-hand with "Y'know?").

2. Moon Unit Zappa's testimony is extremely valuable due to the fact that she, herself, is a *Val.* Thus, what might otherwise have been considered information as seen through the eyes of an objective

onlooker becomes expert testimony from a representative or participant in the *Valley Girl* trend.

3. Words like "brainless," "dumbstruck," "irritating" (in reference to a *Valley Girl* character on a television sitcom), and "vacuous" are just a few of the terms that authors use to refer to *Valley Girls.* Such words clearly depict their contempt for the "trendy, acquisitive culture of the middle class." At one point in the third paragraph, for example, the authors poke fun at girls who cruise malls "buying things and talking their unique kind of trash."

4. Quotes taken from articles in *Newsweek,* a respectable magazine—not simply a music magazine full of the most recent gossip on pop stars—adds legitimacy and credibility to the author's definition of *Valley Girls.* That is, since *Newsweek* does not rely on a single sensational story to sell the magazine (that's not to say there have been exceptions to the rule, of course), it can afford to report information impartially, unemotionally, and accurately. We might consider the quotes from *Newsweek* as voices of detached authority. (Comparing the sort of testimony offered by quoting *Newsweek* to the personal insights on *Valley Girls* presented by Moon Unit Zappa would be a useful discussion point here.)

5. "Valley Girls," presents a progressive exposé defining and explaining the growth and development of the *Val,* a cultural fad that took root in American society during the summer of 1982 and made an about-face three years later for the *Vals* "had a new pioneer of insolent materialism to follow," a person (Madonna) who, according to one sixteen-year-old *Valley Girl* in 1985, "just has everything like the typical dream girl." Such comments about the mutable nature of the *Valley Girl* in the closing paragraph of "Valley Girls" harken back to the essay's controlling idea that the San Fernando Valley "had a moment in the sun"—fleeting though it was.

RICHARD RODRIGUEZ

DOES AMERICA STILL EXIST?

CONTENT

1. Rodriguez claims that America exists everywhere in the city: in the smells, the sights, the sounds, and the pace of its inhabitants. All of these qualities symbolize America.

2. Rodriguez believes that individuality is more important than membership when he states, "We stand together, alone." That is, even though we try to stand together, we do so alone—as individuals—rather than as a united group. Therefore, we reject "total" membership.

3.   The 1960s was the decade that saw the emergence of ethnic pride. As Rodriguez observed, "In the sixties, other groups of Americans learned to champion their rights by analogy to the black civil rights movement." Since that time, the heroic vision of Martin Luther King, Jr. has faded into little more than bureaucratic competition for power.

4.   While Rodriguez states that, "The dream of a single society probably died with *The Ed Sullivan Show*," he goes on to state, "The reality of America persists." To support this claim, Rodriguez shows how teenagers go through high schools in racial groups but tend to assimilate once they graduate and begin working.

STRATEGIES AND STRUCTURES

1.   Answers will vary to all questions.

2.   The author develops his definition of America through abstract discussion, undoubtedly because "abstraction" lends itself more readily to the nature of his argument.

3.   Alluding to the cause and effect and comparison and contrast relationships between immigrants and Americans further assists Rodriguez in developing his definition.

Process Analysis

APPROACHES TO PROCESS ANALYSIS

1. To introduce and start a general discussion of process analysis, bring to class several "how to" books explaining how to paint, how to garden, how to fix a car, how to write a will, how to meditate, how to make love, how to win a lottery, etc. (your college library, undoubtedly, has many such books). Ask students why such books are popular, who buys or uses them, and/or what "how to" book they would feel qualified to write about.

2. Since most of our students major in fields other than English, especially business, engineering, and computer sciences, bring in documents from other disciplines which demonstrate some form of process analysis. For example, focusing on the chronology involved in directive process analysis, you could use an overhead projector to show how the successful completion of a lab experiment depended on following a particular sequence of steps as illustrated in the lab report. Regardless of the discipline you choose as a vehicle for teaching process analysis, it should strongly illustrate the importance of concrete, visual language—as well as the need for transition expressions and linking words—in order to lead your reader smoothly through his/her paper.

GARRISON KEILLOR
How to Write a Personal Letter

CONTENT

1. Basically, Keillor contends that we should write to establish who we are and to show other people that we care about them. Since our

conversations are often vague, we compose letters to expand on our thoughts and to be more direct. Furthermore, one can always return to the written word and reflect upon it, whereas a person is likely to forget large portions of verbal communication.

2. Keillor claims that "some of the best letters are tossed off in a burst of inspiration" since they are not usually motivated by a sense of guilt or obligation—conditions which tend to obstruct the creative process, making it more difficult to write.

3. To begin writing a personal letter, Keillor suggests that you meditate about the person you are writing to.

4. Keillor advises letter writers not to worry about form. Instead, he recommends that one begin with a "simple description of the present moment" and let his or her thoughts flow freely. This way, the fear or uncertainty of not adhering to a "correct" format will not hinder one's writing.

STRATEGIES AND STRUCTURES

1. Though opinions may vary, most students should agree on one point: Keillor is trying to establish a purpose for writing letters—a purpose beyond feelings of guilt or obligation.

2. Just as a "gift" is a token of something special between family and friends, so is a letter according to Keillor. Again, the use of this image stresses the fact that letters are best when they are sent "freely," without a sense of obligation.

3. Keillor obviously believes that "writer's block" is responsible for the lack of correspondence between people, rather than a lack of knowledge about the writing process.

4. Keillor suggests letters are a form of immortality, tying it with his original thesis that a letter allows one "to be known."

JOYCE M. JARRETT

FREEDOM

CONTENT

1. Jarrett is referring to the fact that when she began her journey, she was naive, had no conception of "freedom" and had lived imprisoned "in the poverty-stricken plains" of Georgia. Although many people probably believed that she attended the high school because

she was devoted to the betterment of her people, her curiosity, however, contributed to this illusion because it, and it alone, caused her to attend that high school.

2.   The author went into the school expecting the worst because of what had occurred outside. However, all of the preceding classes proved to be "surprisingly uneventful," and she began to believe that she would be fine. In fact, she was confident enough to "saunter" into her geometry classroom. Her treatment by the students and teacher jarred her back to consciousness and alerted her to the fact that she must begin to be more aware. This incident started her on her long journey to discovering the true meaning of freedom.

3.   The geometry teacher never talks to Jarrett, nor does he use any blatantly racist words. He never admonishes the other members of the class for calling her names; instead, he tells them, "Let's get quiet and make the best of it." His statement immediately notifies her tormentors that he is on their side. He goes even further by making her feel as if she were invisible by not acknowledging her raised hand. Nothing can be more demoralizing.

4.   Jarrett blames herself for that "crushing moment" because she realizes in retrospect that she was too naive to defend herself. The fact that she did not speak out has haunted her all through the years. It did, however, make her much more observant and aided her in her search for freedom. Answers will vary; however, it is hoped that most readers will realize that it was because she was feeling so secure within the walls of that school that she had no accurate conception of freedom.

STRATEGIES AND STRUCTURES

1.   The scene in the geometry classroom provides the climactic moment in this essay, because, like the author, we readers also have been lulled into a false sense of security. We too believe that she will get through the day in an uneventful way. This scene not only serves as a climax but also issues a wake-up call for all of us to be on our toes. She has learned the hard way that she cannot relax her vigilance. Because it is such a blatant reminder of what lies ahead, she now knows that she has to patiently "search" for freedom.

2.   She begins her opening paragraph discussing her "first illusion of freedom." The word illusion helps us to understand that this is a false impression and makes the reader look forward to her being enlightened. Jarrett concludes her essay by stating that "Freedom is not a gift, but a right." We learn that she naively went to this school believing that the Supreme Court's decision had given her freedom.

After a few disturbing incidents outside, she began to believe that she was free once she got within the confines of the school. The most enlightening lesson that she learns is that even though the Supreme Court had liberated her, she "had failed to liberate" herself.

3. Jarrett is an accomplished writer who skillfully leads the reader from her naiveté through her education to the realization that she must work hard to achieve freedom. It is an engrossing tale, in which many of the readers also experience their own naiveté. There is a lesson to be learned here—that even if the courts grant us our freedom, if we don't feel free in our souls, we never will truly be free.

4. Even though Jarrett goes through such a humiliating experience, it becomes evident to the reader just how mature she has become from her years of struggling. She is so adroit at handling her reader that rather than feeling alienated by her, we are outraged at the way she has been treated. Never once does she accuse anyone of inappropriate behavior except herself. By casting all the blame on herself, we immediately feel sympathy for her because we see how human she is.

MALCOLM X

A Homemade Education

CONTENT

1. Malcolm X became extremely frustrated due to his illiteracy, especially when he wanted to write to Mr. Elijah Muhammad. The slang that he knew and used on the streets simply wasn't appropriate to his audience.

2. Starting with the first page of the dictionary, Malcolm X copied it verbatim until he finished the entire dictionary. As he copied the pages, he would read them aloud to himself until he ultimately had broadened his word-base.

3. After copying the first page of the dictionary, Malcolm X felt immensely proud of, not to mention fascinated with, his newly acquired knowledge. Thus, he was inspired to continue copying pages in the dictionary until he had completed the whole book.

4. As a result of Malcolm X's initial desire to improve his writing ability, he became not only a good writer but an avid reader; moreover, a whole new world opened to him, a world he had not been aware of before.

STRATEGIES AND STRUCTURES

1. By starting many of his paragraphs with the first-person pronoun "I," Malcolm X establishes a strong personal voice and shows that education helps create a strong sense of self.

2. Answers will vary.

3. Malcolm X establishes a rhythm by beginning most of his sentences with a subject (usually I) and a verb, which helps to link one paragraph to the next, moving the reader along from this first step he took toward a homemade education to the last.

4. The simple subject–verb patterns sprinkled throughout this essay tend to keep his writing conversational. On the other hand, his education becomes evident through such sentence patterns as "I woke up the next morning, thinking about those words—immensely proud to realize that not only had I written so much at one time, but I'd written words that I never knew were in the world." Like the aforementioned sentence pattern, it is quite apparent that Malcolm X has a complex personality.

LUIS M. VALDEZ

PERSPECTIVES ON 'BORDERS'

CONTENT

1. When Valdez talks about the "brown hordes pouring across the border, the nonborder, this border that cannot hold," he means that no artificially constructed border can stop the natural tendencies of the human race. People will always migrate, crossing the invisible border lines, in order to travel to and live where they want to be. These invisible lines also can never stop the use of a certain language (i.e. Spanish) even though an official language has been declared (English). What he hopes for the future is that all of the cultures will unite to form a "whole vision of humanity," and these borders will not be able to stop this from happening.

2. The controlling idea or thesis of this essay is "There's more to America than just transplanted European culture," which appears in the middle of paragraph three.

3. Answers will vary to this question. It will be interesting to note why students find certain symbols powerful.

4. While both Gómez-Peña and Valdez discuss the issue of borders and border-crossing, Gómez-Peña's essay uses personal experiences to

illustrate his point while Valdez uses a variety of historical facts and cultural symbols to illustrate his ideas. Both essays have an argumentative edge. Valdez uses process analysis to explain how American society is evolving toward a pluralistic one, and in doing so, he argues for it. Gómez-Peña, in describing how others view him, eventually argues for his own definition.

5. Valdez uses the following images: "the sphere, the power of the sun, the power of the planet that pulls from within to hold it together in space," in order to represent different cultures coming together. This humanity must pull us from within and hold us together.

STRATEGIES AND STRUCTURES

1. This essay consists of two parts: (1) the historical background of the Mayan civilization, and (2) the process whereby people of all cultures can come together and create a pluralistic society. Valdez illustrates that America has always been in the process of evolving into a multicultural nation. For instance, the Mayas predicted the coming of the European civilization.

2. Valdez's purpose in the essay is to show how something was done, which he does by explaining and arguing for the process of human and social evolution. As such, he is engaged in informational process analysis. Granted, there is a very strong argumentative edge in this essay; however, expository essays often blend rhetorical modes. Moreover, most compositions have some sort of argumentative edge, usually stated in the thesis or controlling idea.

3. The use of figurative speech, such as similes, in this essay adds to the strong imagery he uses to evoke the readers' emotions. Furthermore, the use of figurative language tends to be creative, complementing the very thing Valdez argues for: an ongoing act of creation.

4. While students will respond to the last two parts of this question differently, they will probably have something to say about how Valdez's vision of the future rests on speculation. However, if we look into the past and see a precedent—the accomplishments of Mayan society—by extension, we might theorize that anything is possible.

5. Valdez's use of contractions, simple and compound sentences, fragments, asides, and direct addresses to the audience are all characteristic of spoken English. However, different readers will have varying responses as to whether they interfere with the reader. One might point out, for example, that fragmented sentences create choppiness. On the other hand, many people won't even notice the fragments because the powerful images themselves function as links between the various ideas.

JESSICA MITFORD

BEHIND THE FORMALDEHYDE CURTAIN

CONTENT

1. Formaldehyde is a compound used chiefly as a disinfectant and preservative.

2. Embalming is a process in which the "blood is drained out through veins and replaced by embalming fluid pumped in through the arteries." She notes that every mortician has a favorite injection point for the embalming fluid. After the veins have been drained, "About three to six gallons of a dyed and perfumed solution of formaldehyde, glycerin, borax, phenol, alcohol and water . . ." are pumped through the body. After that the contents of the body are "pumped out and replaced with 'cavity fluid.'" Since the only reason for embalming is to preserve a corpse so that others may view it before it is buried, the author is outraged at the practice. Furthermore, embalming and restorative art are "so universally employed in the United States and Canada that the funeral director does it routinely, without consulting corpse and kin." She also notes the fact that there is no law requiring permission to embalm one's deceased relative thereby calling into question the ethics of funeral directors.

3. "About three to six gallons of a dyed and perfumed solution of formaldehyde, glycerin, borax, phenol, alcohol and water . . ." are pumped through the body.

4. There is a five-part process that happens to the body between entering a mortuary and being lowered into the grave: embalming, restoring, casketing, viewing and the funeral, and finally burial.

STRATEGIES AND STRUCTURES

1. Mitford's use of irony and sarcasm denote her disdain for the funeral industry. The use of irony enables the reader to see two sides of Mitford. On one hand, we have the author using informational process analysis to explain what happens to a corpse when it enters a mortuary. On the other hand, we see Mitford, who finds such practices deplorable and unethical. The important thing to remember is that she is not cold and heartless about such a sensitive subject as death. If anything, she believes that the dead deserve dignity and respect in that people—before death—should have the right to choose what will happen after they die.

2. Mitford's analysis clearly outlines a process she feels is overly complex and unnecessary. By using this informational process she is

able to describe the superfluous practices employed by funeral directors. Answers will vary in the two final parts of this question.

3. In contrast to Yorick's skull, which is bone and has been allowed to decay naturally, its counterpart has been "sprayed, sliced, pierced, pickled, trussed, trimmed, creamed, waxed, painted, rouged, and neatly dressed—transformed from a common corpse into a beautiful memory picture."

4. Mitford quotes textbooks on embalming to help her explain the embalming process as well as to illustrate some of the absurd advice by the so-called experts.

Comparison and Contrast

APPROACHES TO COMPARISON AND CONTRAST

1. Assign students the task of reading the want ads at home, requesting that they reach some sort of conclusion about the items in a particular column (e.g., houses for sale, rooms for rent, or the most promising employment prospects) by asking questions like "Which is better?" "Which is more reasonable?" "Why is one item in a column preferable to another?" (Don't request them to specifically compare and contrast; the fact that students know and frequently use this method of reasoning to arrive at conclusions should be saved for a short "mini-lesson" in class.)

2. To visually introduce students to the expository value of comparison/contrast, select two paintings dealing with similar subjects (landscapes, ocean scenes, portraits) but developed using different artistic styles (realism, abstraction, surrealism). For example, you might select Da Vinci's "Mona Lisa" and Klee's "Head of a Man." Now, along with your students, develop a list of similarities between the two paintings and a second list denoting the differences. Next, explain how an art critic might use the same strategy of comparison/ contrast to evaluate an artist's work (e.g., "Leedom's painting is innovative but lacks the physiological complexity of Dali").

ANDREW LAM
THEY SHUT MY GRANDMOTHER'S ROOM DOOR

CONTENT

1. The door in Lam's essay symbolizes not only the passage from life to death, but also a bureaucratic effort to shield death from the convalescent patients.

2. The grandmother's life in Vietnam was unified (e.g., birth and death both occurred at home). In contrast, her life in the United States is more "disjointed." She is not dying in her own bed at home surrounded by family or friends; rather, she is in a hospital surrounded by people she doesn't know.

3. Vietnamese culture, according to Lam, is filled with pain and agony. It "stares death in the face." American culture, on the other hand, emphasizes pleasure and escapism. Nowhere is the contrast between cultures better illustrated than when he points out that "While Vietnamese holidays are based on death anniversaries, birthdays are celebrated here [the United States]."

4. People in America deal with their fear of dying by making death as pleasant as possible.

STRATEGIES AND STRUCTURES

1. Both the opening and final paragraphs contain images that contrast Vietnam with America, emphasizing the point that both cultures are different. The image of the door appears in both paragraphs, bringing the essay full circle and creating a sense of closure.

2. Lam gathers information for his essay from his personal experiences (e.g., his experiences with his grandmother) and his observations of others (e.g., his observations of the convalescent patients).

3. Lam uses very clear topic sentences to organize and unify the progression of his essay. Such sentences establish a definite focus—the discussion point—for each paragraph, which he then develops with specific examples.

4. Lam uses many specific examples to illustrate his points. For example, he states that convalescent homes remind us of how the elderly suffer. The author illustrates this idea with the examples of an elderly man who can no longer play the piano because of arthritis. Lam's other examples vividly contrast the differences between America and Vietnam. Overall, his effective use of concrete details leaves an indelible impression on the reader.

SUZANNE BRITT

NEAT PEOPLE VS. SLOPPY PEOPLE

CONTENT

1. Using humor, Britt, at once, attacks the reliability of a negative stereotype (sloppy person) and pokes fun at the rigid standards people use to criticize others. Intentionally, of course, she herself is guilty of judging others with strict standards.

2. Since everyone knows at least one neat and one sloppy person, Britt believes that she and her readers share a common ground. Thus, Britt is assured that her audience will appreciate her amusing treatment of stereotypes.

3. From the opening line, "Neat people are lazier and meaner than sloppy people," to the closing statement, neat people ". . . send their children off to boarding school (too many scuffmarks on the hardwood floors)," the negative characteristics Britt attributes to "neat people" clearly indicate where her sympathies lie. She identifies with sloppy people.

4. Britt asserts that neat people always buy items in small amounts and always throw such things as a newspaper in the trash—long before it ever has a chance of becoming scattered around the house (after 7:05 A.M.).

STRATEGIES AND STRUCTURES

1. The function of Britt's humor in this essay is primarily to entertain her reader while satirizing humanity's tendency to stereotype.

2. The repetition of the same opening words in many of her paragraphs keeps the reader focused on the topic and creates a sense of unity. More important, however, is how Britt structures her paragraphs that begin with the same words. While she begins only three paragraphs—early in the essay—with *sloppy people,* she concludes her essay with six consecutive paragraphs beginning with *neat people.* Such emphasis on the negativity of a positive social quality clearly indicates the cruel, inexact nature of stereotypes.

3. Extremes are usually absurd and ridiculous and provide her with material for many humorous anecdotes. Moreover, the nature of extremes applies equally well to stereotypes and stereotyping; both are absurd. Our tendency to generalize is, in part, what Britt is criticizing, and many inexperienced writers tend to use generalization to prop up ideas that have not been carefully thought out. General-

izations do not undermine the quality of Britt's writing because she is not expecting her readers to take them seriously.

4. Britt is contrasting rather than comparing neat and sloppy people to illustrate that people who stereotype tend to focus on *differences* between people, places, religions, and cultures rather than *similarities.*

URSULA LE GUIN

AMERICAN SF AND THE OTHER

CONTENT

1. The cultural and the racial alien are most readily recognized as "The Other" in the world in general and science fiction in particular. Refer students to recent election issues related to immigration, and ask them to consider how frequently the terms *legal* and *illegal* aliens appeared (and continue to appear) in news, whether printed, broadcast, or on-line. The qualification "legal" is rather ridiculous, of course; the *alien* or "The Other" is different from the status quo—perhaps in terms of the controlling gender, cultural traditions, or language. The ever-present paranoia of "The Other," propelling the notion that to curtail the evolution of new social orders, whether they originate in other galaxies or local communities, clearly support the "old pulp concern" and feelings toward aliens: *the only good alien is a dead alien.*

2. From Mary Shelley's *Frankenstein,* considered by many to be the first modern piece of science fiction, to the present, *science fiction* has constantly concerned itself with the future: future lifestyles, future threats—byproducts of so-called progress, and future enlightenment, something one would expect from an advanced civilization. Ironically, little compassion and wisdom is perceived in most futuristic stories. Intergalactic empires, always seeking power and dominance—constantly at war with each other, are common plot lines (give or take a princess and a space pilot or two). This is why Le Guin claims that most science fiction has been "incredibly regressive and unimaginative." It tends to eclipse the importance of intelligence and understanding because in an aggressive, hostile universe, might makes right, and should make us wonder whether science fiction is at all civilized.

3. Answers will vary here, though most students will probably detect her irritability with fellow science fiction writers for perpetuating regressive rather than progressive human behavior in their futuristic

stories. Perhaps Le Guin acutely feels "The Other" in science fiction because she, herself, is an author of imaginative fiction. Moreover, she is a woman and painfully aware of the subservient, insignificant roles assigned to women in most SF.

4. The result of denying any affinity to and declaring your difference from many kinds of people may well be *self-alienation* because denial often leads to an "impoverished" sense of reality. In a state of spiritual deadness, therefore, "the only possible relationships are a power relationship."

5. American *science fiction* has tended to favor a "hierarchy of superiors and inferiors, with rich, ambitious, aggressive males at the top, a great gap, and then at the bottom the poor, the uneducated, the faceless masses, and all the women." In other words, the world of *science fiction* presents a rarely changing social order, an order that does not empower people; instead, it subjugates them to their "betters." America carries the mystique—if not promise—of being a "land of opportunity" (e.g., anyone can become rich, famous, powerful, and popular). Since upward social mobility, the American Dream, would not be possible in a fixed social order, then, in theory, all fixed societies would be considered "unAmerican."

STRATEGIES AND STRUCTURES

1. After informing the reader in her opening paragraph that "the very low status of women in SF should make us ponder whether SF is civilized at all," Le Guin moves on to the second where she expands her opening comments and phrases the controlling idea or thesis of "SF and The Other" in the form of a rhetorical question—a question she intends to thoroughly answer in the body of her essay: "Isn't the 'subjection of women' in SF merely a symptom of a whole which is authoritarian power-worshipping, and intensely parochial?"

2. Answers will vary here. You might point out to your students, however, that *science fiction* functions as an umbrella for a genre consisting of many subdivisions. To distinguish the varied forms of *science fiction,* authors and "sci fi" buffs refer to a specific acronym; for instance, SF refers to *science fiction;* H alludes to *horror;* F represents fantasy or fantastic literature, and so on.

3. One at a time, Le Guin examines different aspects of "The Other," personas she refers to as aliens in relationship to science fiction. There is the "sexual Alien, and the social Alien, and the cultural Alien, and finally the racial Alien." Her strategy for comparing conventions of science fiction and "The Other," include division and classification as well as a strong sense of definition.

4. Larry Niven, who wrote "The Inconstant Moon," from *All the Myriad Ways* (1971); Stanley Weinbaum, author of *A Martian Chronology;* and Cyril Kornbluth, Ted Sturgeon, and Cordwainer Smith—writers who all followed Weinbaum's lead and wrote about the "sympathetic alien"—are all cited at one time or another in Le Guin's essay. By referring to more than one male author of science fiction, Le Guin manages to illustrate that her comments about them are representative rather than selective. It is interesting to note that even in the case of presenting "The Other" as a "sympathetic alien," women science fiction authors are not cited. You might ask your students why they think she chooses to keep the focus of her essay away from female science fiction writers.

5. Although Le Guin concerns herself with demonstrating that most individuals portrayed in science fiction—regardless of sex, heritage, social standing, or appearance—are not depicted as people as much as a "thing," she both begins and concludes her composition referring to women as victims of an authoritative, male elite. Le Guin's conclusion also makes a call for action, as she states that it is high time that writers and readers of science fiction "stopped daydreaming about a return to the age of Queen Victoria, and started thinking about the future," a future where men and women indulge a bit more in human idealism and a lot less in power struggles.

MICHAEL T. KAUFMAN

KISSING CUSTOMS

CONTENT

1. Kaufman was self-conscious about kissing hands because it was not the social custom of the United States. Secondly, he was afraid of what his "feminist friends back home might have said." As he pointed out, his feminist friends would not have wanted him "to kiss the hands of all women simply because they were women."

2. The Polish people took up hand kissing as an act of rebellion against the Communist regime. It symbolizes the tradition of dukes and barons which was a custom before the Communists took over.

3. Kaufman would alter the way he kissed women's hands depending upon their ages. For instance, he would bring a young girl's hand to his lips; for older women he would bring "his lips to her hands." If he couldn't tell, he would then treat them as if they were young. As he pointed out, "Sometimes you can play out little dramas."

4. The real advantage of hand kissing "was that it provided a ritual that enriched the routine of everyday life." Americans are not ready for hand kissing because they lack self-discipline and confidence and may insult feminists. He feels Americans could "affirm something less than intimacy but more than passing acquaintance" by shaking hands.

STRATEGIES AND STRUCTURES

1. Kaufman uses the basic block method of comparing and contrasting specific customs of greetings in the United States and Poland. Answers to the second question will vary.

2. The author uses specific examples and observations to illustrate the differences between the two societies. For example, he discusses his own kissing practices in Poland with the way a waiter greets customers at a restaurant in America.

3. Kaufman writes very matter-of-factly without being frivolous or accusative. As a result, the way he conveys his material is light as opposed to heavy-handed. Also many of his anecdotes have a humorous tone.

4. The author obviously approves of the Polish custom of hand kissing; therefore, he contrasts this custom with the American way of greeting people, shaking hands, which he feels is insensitive. This suggests that no rhetorical mode is pure and that a combination of rhetorical strategies is used to achieve one's purpose.

5. In translation, *Tant pis* means "That is our loss," or "So much the worse for us." Though Kaufman had learned to express himself through rituals accepted and respected by a foreign society, he reverts to boorishness—and his former non-expressive self—once he returns to the United States. He certainly does not feel like a better, more enriched person by forsaking simple gestures of respect that had become a way of life for him while in Poland.

E. B. WHITE

EDUCATION

CONTENT

1. The controlling idea of this essay is essentially that country schools provide a better, more *natural* learning environment than city schools. White says he has always preferred public (country)

schools to private (city) schools and establishes the logical and ethical basis for his preferences early in the essay. For instance, the entire first paragraph is devoted to explaining how and why he holds his son's country school teacher in such high esteem.

2. The formal experiences White refers to tend to be cold, superficial, almost clinical encounters with city life and education. The bus, for instance, sucks "the boy in" like an angry, growling steel beast. He was "worked on" by a half a dozen teachers every day (very impersonal). His great academic accomplishments included making "Indian weapons of a semi-deadly nature." And when people got sick at school, there were periods of *incubation and allied magic.*

3. White's son wore "overalls and an old sweater" when he attended the private school in the city, and he "dressed in corduroys, sweatshirt, and short rubber boots" when he went to the public school in the country. Both modes of dress may seem rather casual, though a sweater would probably be considered more classy than a sweatshirt. Student answers to the last part of this question will undoubtedly vary, but how and why they reached their conclusions might prove to be a fruitful class discussion.

4. As White says in the opening paragraph, he has the utmost respect and admiration for his son's country school teacher who "not only undertakes to instruct her charges in all the subjects of the first three grades, but she manages to function quietly and effectively as a guardian of health, their clothes, their habits, their mothers, and their snowball engagements." The country teacher shares confidences with students; White's son, in fact, considers his country teacher one of his best friends. In short, the country teacher sounds like a well-rounded, warm-hearted, caring human being. In contrast, instead of having a single teacher who can do almost everything for the students, city teachers seem cold, reserved, specialized, and impersonal. In the city, White's son was taught by "a half dozen teachers," cared for by a "nurse," supervised by an "athletic instructor," and fed meals prepared by a "dietitian." Country teachers seem particularly worldly and wise, while city teachers seem to have limited knowledge and little compassion.

5. Answers will vary to this question.

STRATEGIES AND STRUCTURES

1. White discusses country schools with reverence and respect. His sardonic tone definitely reflects the disregard—if not disdain—which he holds for city schools, schools where nothing really productive happens. "It was an electric, colorful, regimented, existence. . . ," almost contrary to normal human needs and behavior.

2. Answers may vary a good deal on this question. White himself says he suspects that his bias is partially an attempt to justify "his own past" because he never really knew anything but public (country) schools. His wife, in contrast, had never known anything but private (city) schools. Students might note that although the family, as a whole, was concerned about the move from a city to a country school, White's individual bias might have put him at ease.

3. The author uses irony to contrast what one would expect to be the superior learning environment (the city school with its specialists in learning, health, nutrition—and its modern plumbing) to an environment which seems lacking in essentials (a country school with its two-room schoolhouse for six grade levels, chemical toilet in the basement, all-purpose, renaissance woman instructor who can do everything). The fact that one of his son's major achievements as "the scholar" was learning how to get attention by fainting like the child in the Christmas play is a prime example of the shallow, insignificant depth of his city learning.

4. Block comparison tends to predominate in this essay. With the exception of the first part of paragraph 2, which contrasts White's learning experiences with his wife's and presents their concern about moving from "a medium-priced private institution with semi-progressive ideas of education . . . ," paragraphs 2 and 3 discuss private or city schools and paragraphs 4 and 5 contrast them to public or country schools. The final paragraph looks at both schools in retrospect, and implies that the education White's son received at the country school was more substantial than that of a progressive city school.

5. Something that is lightning quick lasts but a few seconds. Here White's son says that the main difference between attending school in the country as opposed to the city is that "the day seems to go by much quicker in the country," implying that one is definitely more interesting—possibly more educational—than the other. This, of course, echoes White's own experience and validates the bias he talked about in the second paragraph.

Division and Classification

APPROACHES TO DIVISION AND CLASSIFICATION

1. Dividing and classifying is sometimes such a natural technique that many instructors never bother teaching it as a separate theoretical mode. Likewise, students are familiar with it as the five-paragraph essay. Regardless, a quick way to refresh students' memories on a strategy they all are probably familiar with would be to use "subject trees" to visually represent the division and classification of the subject. Begin by listing a subject and its parts on the overhead. For example, an instructor could start with the topic "relatives" and list words such as: aunt, uncle, grandmother, grandfather, brother, sister, mother, father, brother-in-law, sister-in-law, guardian, etc. Then the instructor would classify these into three categories:

IMMEDIATE	EXTENDED	FAMILY BY MARRIAGE
mother	aunt	brother-in-law
father	uncle	sister-in-law
sister	grandmother	mother-in-law
brother	grandfather	father-in-law

2. If you would like to give your students practice in taking notes and organizing them into a logical structure, use the following mini-lesson. Give a ten-minute talk on material your students are not totally familiar with. Have at least three major divisions to your presentation with plenty of examples, some of which you may want to write on the board. Do not present your material in chronological order. In other words, disorganize the three parts of the

62

presentation. Then, have the students get into small groups and discuss the notes they have taken. Have them piece together the main points of the lecture and outline them using emphatic order.

MARTIN LUTHER KING, JR.

THE WAYS OF MEETING OPPRESSION

CONTENT

1. The three ways people deal with their oppressions are: acceptance, violence, and nonviolent resistance.

2. Some people simply "give up" because they have been oppressed so long they just don't feel like fighting oppression anymore. Such individuals hurt everyone because, "To accept passively an unjust system is to cooperate with that system; thereby the oppressed become as evil as the oppressor."

3. Using violence as a means to achieving justice ". . . is impractical because it is a descending spiral ending in destruction for all. . . . It is immoral because it seeks to humiliate the opponent rather than win his understanding; it seeks to annihilate rather than convert."

4. Nonviolent resistance is preferable to violence or doing nothing in order to overcome oppression because the African-American can enlist "all men of good will in his struggle for equality." Moreover, "nonviolent resistance is not aimed against oppressors but against oppression."

STRATEGIES AND STRUCTURES

1. For the first part of the essay, King's historical references indicate that acceptance never improves the lives of oppressed people. He later shows that those who used violence (both impractical and immoral) to escape from tyranny or oppression destroyed communities and made "brotherhood impossible." His final discussion of nonviolent resistance concluded by saying "under its banner consciences, not racial groups, are enlisted."

2. Each division allows the reader to thoroughly concentrate on one type of resistance to oppression at a time. This way the reader does not confuse the qualities of one method of resistance with another.

3. King places his material in emphatic order. That is to say, he saves the type of resistance he advocates until last for discussion. With this order what he contends is the solution to oppression leaves a lasting impression in his reader's mind.

CONSTANCE GARCÍA-BARRIO

CREATURES THAT HAUNT THE AMERICAS

CONTENT

1. Most of the creatures García-Barrio describes originated in Africa where they, being invisible, sneaked aboard slave ships headed to the "New World."

2. The creatures which "haunt" the Americas have supernatural origins and a mischievous nature in common.

3. Since the "Blacks and Indians" were always fighting with each other and the moans of dying men disturbed him, the devil decided to exterminate both races to get some "peace and quiet." However, he met "a lively, buxom Esmeraldeña before doing so, ". . . married her and settled down, as much as the devil can ever settle." The result of their union was the Tunda.

4. Answers will vary here.

STRATEGIES AND STRUCTURES

1. The opening paragraph informs the reader on how creatures from African folktales got to the Americas. The general thesis of this essay is rather straightforward: "When Africans reached the New World, the creatures stepped on shore with them." The bulk of the essay classifies the different creatures that came aboard slave ships to the *New World*, discussing them in relationship to their new surroundings.

2. García-Barrio helps her readers envision the creatures she writes about by using descriptive details, creating distinct images. Some of the images she casts include: "a fat, ugly little man with more hair all over than hell has bedevilment"; "little black men who wear no clothes" and have frogheads; "a deformed black woman with huge lips and clubfoot"; and the Lobisón (wolfman) which has "a wolf's body and a pig's head."

3. The creatures in this essay fall into one of two categories: those that haunt children (e.g., Hairy man, guije, Tunda) or those that haunt adults (e.g., Ciguapa, Lobisón, ghosts). García-Barrio undoubtedly wanted to show the wide range of folk characters (not just stories to scare or amuse children) that came to the *New World* from Africa.

4. The final paragraph points out an issue which has become rather apparent after reading García-Barrio's essay: ". . . black folk tales bring to light sometimes forgotten cultural treasures Africans brought to the Americas." Student responses to some of the other

possible purposes for the type of concluding paragraph she wrote will vary.

ROBERTSON DAVIES
A FEW KIND WORDS FOR SUPERSTITION

CONTENT

1. Despite discrediting claims by modern science, superstition, which has been with us "for as long as we have any chronicle of human behavior," is still prevalent today even "among people who are indisputably rational and learned."

2. Vain observances is an appropriate title because the rituals which have been repeated by people for thousands of years lack substance or worth (e.g., Does the throwing of salt over the left shoulder "hit the Devil in the eye" when the Devil's existence has not been conclusively proven?). Answers will vary for examples of observances of superstition in childhood.

3. Few people will admit to superstition because "it implies naivete or ignorance." Superstition also is associated with our pagan, prehistoric roots and the Devil.

4. In our modern scientific and technological world, all of us are trying to find ways to know and control our fates. I Ching and oracles attempt to give us answers and to tell us how to do just that.

STRATEGIES AND STRUCTURES

1. Answers will vary as to what kind of superstition is most common. Davies divides and classifies superstition into four categories which are: acts such as not walking under ladders, consulting oracles, the use of "bringers of luck," and attempts to bribe deities in order to achieve good luck.

2. According to Davies, the four divisions of superstition are: 1) Vain Observations, 2) Divination, 3) Idolatry, and 4) Improper Worship of the True God. Answers will vary as to any other division he might have made.

3. Even though the author considers himself modern and educated, he is just as superstitious as the rest of humanity and wanted all the help he could get to pass his exams when he was in college.

4. Because they are more learned and scientific, professors who act superstitiously would be more of an anomaly than farmers.

GARY TEWALESTEWA

AMERICAN INDIANS: HOMELESS IN THEIR OWN HOMELAND

CONTENT

1. One of the major causes contributing to the growing number of homeless Native Americans is that they refuse to take refuge because they do not feel accepted by the general population. In addition, the U.S. government refuses to acknowledge any serious problem.

2. Tewalestewa contends that the conflict between two social systems (philosophies), one based on the ". . . accumulation of land wealth, mass profit, and individual competition," and the other system based on "a cooperative, spiritual, and communal way of life," is the ". . . root of the increasing numbers of American Indians becoming homeless."

3. Native Americans feel inferior because they have been degraded by and isolated from society. Also, for the last hundred years the government has been attempting to destroy any sense of identity which ties them to "spiritual and cooperative cultural forms" within their tribal society. At the same time, "Their need for decent housing, education, nutritious food, real jobs, and programs that really work has steadily increased and the demand has not been met" by the government.

4. Answers will vary.

STRATEGIES AND STRUCTURES

1. Tewalestewa's title immediately calls into question a favorite American axiom which states the United States is a land with "liberty and justice for all."

2. The four divisions of this essay would be: 1) the statement of purpose along with statistics, 2) historical background, 3) the competition between homeless people, and 4) a call to action in which the author requests that all Native Americans live as they were meant to live and "be Indian."

3. The word capitalist has a negative connotation in this essay and represents the motivating force which lies behind many of the injustices inflicted upon Native Americans throughout history: greed.

ROBERT BLY

MEN'S INITIATION RITES

CONTENT

1. A spiral repeats a pattern, and like the four seasons constantly running into each other, the four stages of male initiation rites have a circular movement. In contrast, a "walk down a road" does not conclude where it began. Instead, a "walk down a road" denotes a forward progression, a journey moving from one point to another—but never back to the point of departure.

2. Bly addresses any interested reader in general—but, eventually, men in particular in "Men's Initiation Rites." With a few minor exceptions, however, Bly does not use the first person plural point of view until the first paragraph in "The Invisible Czarina," the final section of his essay. Up until that time, he speaks about male initiation rites from a third person point of view. By the second sentence in the final paragraph, Bly clearly identifies his primary audience: men. There he states that "as men, we go through all stages in a shallow way, then go back, live in several stages at once, go through them all with slightly less shallowness, return again to our parents, bond and separate once more, find a new male mother, and so on and so on."

3. Student answers will vary to this question. For class discussion, you might have your classes analyze the nature of "*things that impress us.*" Once the class has divided and classified *impressive characteristics* of people, places, situations, and things, have everyone return to his/her response to content question #3 in Bly's essay and determine where it would fit under the "*things that impress us*" list that was generated by the entire class.

4. Bly contends that our culture (especially American culture), lacks the institution of the "male mother and has actually dropped any memory of it" into forgetfulness. Instead of experiencing a second birth where the initiate symbolically is "freed from his bonds to his mother and his father" by placing "his head, or consciousness, into the hands of an older man he trusts, males in our culture tend to receive a single birth of the mother. What does this mean? To put it simply, by overlooking the symbolic ritual with the *male mother archetype,* many men are never freed from bonds that attach them to both parents.

5. The variety of responses will be quite diverse here and may well be worth a roundtable class discussion, noting how, why, when, and where they have observed males going through one of the initiation

stages Bly mentions. Personal responses to content question #5 may also provide students with an opportunity to individually brainstorm the topic of male initiations prior to group activities.

STRATEGIES AND STRUCTURES

1.   Likening "Men's Initiation Rites" to the four seasons in a year, Bly further contends that the four seasons amount to four stages in male development—stages of events which are cyclical in nature, running into and repeating each other. The specific stages or events Bly classifies include: 1) *Bonding with and Separation from Mother;* 2) *Bonding with and Separation from Father;* 3) *Male Mother; and The Invisible Czarina.*

2.   "Men's Initiation Rites," the title of Bly's essay, concisely and clearly announces his subject matter. With these three words, Bly is able to convey enough material to allow readers to make initial predictions about the essay. The title may also spark reader curiosity or interest. Take a moment or so to discuss the potential significance of a title in an essay. (As a follow-up to this question, have students take a look at the table of contents for *Visions Across the Americas* and make other predictions based on an essay's title.) At the same time, you might discuss the potential hazards of expecting a title, alone, to serve as the thesis of an essay.

3.   Opinions will vary greatly here. However, it is less important that students agree or disagree about the effectiveness of Bly's "lead-in" sentences than to be able to justify their points of view. True, discussing the diverse student responses to this question will be profitable, but you should also take this opportunity to engage in an exercise designed to build dexterity and clarity in opening paragraphs. Have your students return to one of their essays, and rework its opening paragraph—adding or revising "lead-in" sentences which lead to a focused thesis. Then have your students take the same "focused thesis," and "lead-in" to it using different, completely new, sentences. You might expand this exercise into a group activity where each person shares his or her three versions of the same thesis paragraph.

4.   Students will, no doubt, have a variety of responses to this question (you might want to highlight the common thread or threads of their responses). Bly's simple diction keeps his readers focused on his thesis in general and the divisions of it—male initiation rites—in particular. Excessively difficult vocabulary could easily distract and confuse readers. As it stands, Bly's simple vocabulary and the density of his subject matter work harmoniously toward promoting clear exposition rather than against each other.

5. Strategically, by referring to a broad range of male initiation rites drawn from cultures throughout the world, Bly endeavors to demonstrate that the rites he categorizes are representative of the male gender—not men from a particular regional, social, economic, religious, or ethnic group. Multiple examples of male initiations also narrow the inductive leap in logic if and when Bly's discussion points *seem* questionable.

9

CAUSE AND Effect

APPROACHES TO CAUSE AND EFFECT

1. After printing the word "why" in large letters on the blackboard, ask students to carefully consider the ramifications of the word. Then, have them write three complex sentences which logically express the reason(s) why something happened or happens (causes), and three complex sentences commenting on the result or results of an incident (effects). Using student examples, proceed to discuss the cause-and-effect relationships and their strategic purpose in expository writing from whatever pedagogical view you deem most beneficial. This might also be a good opportunity to demonstrate the importance of subordinate conjunctions in establishing a logical explanation or argument (critical thinking).

2. Devise some sort of activity which would end in a situation wherein you ask the class why something happened—a lead-in to a discussion of *causes*. You might get some students to be your accomplices here. For instance, you could choreograph a conversation between yourself and a student or between two students that ends in a loud verbal argument, culminating with someone throwing something at the wall. While the dramatic intensity of such an approach to causation may make some students initially uncomfortable, they'll be relieved after you assure them that the entire incident was prearranged. In the meantime, the entire class has a common experience to critically assess in terms of cause-and-effect relationships.

MEGAN McGUIRE

GROWING UP WITH TWO MOMS

CONTENT

1. When McGuire found out that her mother was gay, she felt that her family, all of a sudden, was no longer *normal*. She felt she needed to lie about her mom. Ironically, McGuire was never part of an all-American family—if, indeed such a family unit even exists outside television reruns of *Leave It to Beaver*, *The Cosby Show*, and *The Brady Bunch*. Her parents separated when she was only five years old, so she and her brother had to split their time between their parents. Meanwhile, their father remarried, and their mother dated men. Thus, they "assumed their parents were straight."

2. McGuire wanted to be popular, so she "laughed at the jokes about gays." When she entered high school, McGuire also wanted to join numerous clubs, but she was paranoid that everything she "gained socially would disappear if anyone ever found out that while they went home after volleyball practice to their Brady Bunch dinners with mom and dad," she would go home to "two moms."

3. In paragraph five, McGuire reflected upon the fact that her home life was not unlike that of her friends who grew up in straight families. McGuire's family had "meetings, fights, trips and dinners." She even notes that she and her brother eventually accepted Barb as a second mother.

4. McGuire credits a "really great counselor and a friend who had an "it's not a big deal and I knew it anyway attitude," for helping her to come to terms and become comfortable with her "two mom family." She even went so far as to allow her local newspaper to interview her for an article being written about "gay families." She suffered some peer abuse as a result of the interview, but she also created much curiosity among the "kids."

5. Following the speech McGuire delivered on her school's National Coming Out Day, she lost some friends. Other individuals made rude remarks to her, yet she says "that only made me stronger." She realized that "the hardest thing to deal with is other people's ignorance, not the family part." If anything, McGuire hoped that she was blazing a path for other children who, like herself, felt "scared" and "alone" growing up with a gay parent. Like their own mother, Barb encouraged McGuire and her brother to excel in school. She also helped to support the family unit when their mother went to college to earn her Ph.D. in public health—the sort of loving gesture any spouse or significant other might make.

STRATEGIES AND STRUCTURES

1. The author employs narration and description to express how she felt growing up with two mothers. Narration allows her to also convey the chronology of events that led her from an initial sense that it was not fair that her mother was "one of 'those' people," to the realization that her upbringing in a gay family was harmful and hurtful mostly because of "other people's ignorance."

2. McGuire's essay projects a tone of sincerity, and this is particularly important as she explains her initial reaction when she learned her mother was gay, her feeling that she had to hide the fact that she had "two moms" from her friends, and her ultimate acceptance of her mother's lifestyle.

3. The pathos that evolved out of McGuire's experiences as a child of gay parents—two moms—impresses readers far more than a detailed, theoretical discussion of human nature. Human beings are not machines: rather, they are complex organisms that simply do not respond to emotionally charged situations with detachment and cool objectivity. McGuire expresses shame and fears when she realizes that her mother is gay. In fact, she thinks she must hide the truth about her home life and her mother's sexual preference from her friends. Spin off this question in a class discussion by having students explain some of the ways they have responded to an event or person who seems to threaten their orderly view of the world (e.g., hearing about a friend's death, receiving low marks on an examination, discovering someone you trusted had betrayed you, and so on).

4. Answers will vary here, possibly depending on your students' awareness and acceptance of gay culture. Perhaps a student will be impressed by McGuire's firsthand testimony that—apart from her phobias perpetuated by intolerant, ignorant, or exploitive members of society—her upbringing really did not differ that much from friends who grew up with straight parents.

5. This question will invite numerous responses, some grounded in the notion that an essay should consist of five paragraphs and others based on the fact that, with all of its joys, fears, traumas, and epiphanies, the complexity of human nature deserves more detailed attention. As a critical thinking exercise, you might spend some time going over the reasoning behind their responses.

KAREN RAY

The Naked Face

CONTENT

1. Since Ray rubs her eyes, has a baby daughter who constantly has her hands all over the author's face, and fears that "removing makeup would go the same way as scrubbing the sink and cleaning the oven," she pragmatically reasons why she is most comfortable wearing a "naked face." Philosophically, Ray dislikes excessive use of makeup since too much artifice conceals the real person.

2. The author discusses the history of cosmetic use in order to show how the use of artifice always has been popular with the human race for one reason or another. For instance, she discusses how prehistoric man tattooed his body in order to conjure up the fierce qualities of animals or simply for camouflage. At times, people used cosmetics (such as rouge) to hide blemishes (e.g., scars from the pox), or they wore perfume to hide body odors since bathing was rather unpopular.

3. As mentioned above, prehistoric man tattooed himself to enhance his natural beauty.

4. In her essay, Ray offers evidence that beauty is influenced by fashion when she discusses how "during the 19th century, unadorned innocence was the height of fashion. Intricate hair styles and colors were out of fashion and lip coloring was thought to be downright vulgar." Another example from 18th-century England states, "fashionable woman (and man, too) wore false eyebrows made of mouseskin."

5. While responses to this question may vary a bit, Ray does point out that "pearlized" lipstick now contains an artificial substance in place of fish scales.

STRATEGIES AND STRUCTURES

1. Obviously, the opening sentence is meant to be an attention-getter that stimulates the reader's curiosity to read on.

2. Specific examples are effective in this essay because they allow the author to talk about her subject in concrete terms which allow the reader to visualize as well as intellectualize what Ray is talking about.

3. Actually, the fragments in paragraph 2 are merely items on a list of cosmetics. Since her objective is not necessarily for us to see how these cosmetics work in relationship to each other, her point of introducing us to them is achieved briefly and bluntly.

4. In a humorous fashion, Ray indicates that she feels somewhat ambivalent towards cosmetics. Though she takes a serious look at ridiculous notions, such as, the complete woman is not seen without her make-up, Ray does recognize that throughout history there have been both practical and fashionable reasons for using cosmetics. Thus, the author really passes no final judgment on the issue of cosmetic use; she seems to feel that, ultimately, using make-up should be a matter of personal preference—not convention.

5. By stating that she is proud of her strong fingernails, that she has been thinking of showing them off a bit more than she's done in the past, and that she is planning to get a manicure "one of these days," Ray suggests that despite what she has said about being a "nudist" from the neck up today, she may change her philosophy about cosmetic use tomorrow.

ALLENE GUSS GROGNET

ELDERLY REFUGEES AND LANGUAGE LEARNING

CONTENT

1. The author states that many factors contribute to language learning by the elderly. If the person is unhealthy, his or her ability will be affected (e.g., hearing and vision loss). The elderly refugee faces even more problems; he or she considers himself or herself old at a much earlier age (mid-forties), and Asians feel they should not attempt new languages in their old age. While prepubescent children are better at mimicry—possibly because of cerebral elasticity—older learners have the benefit of "neural cells responsible for higher order linguistic process, such as understanding semantic relationships and grammatical sensitivity. . . ."

2. As mentioned above, physical health is one of the factors; the others include: mental health, cultural expectations, and individual attitudes and motivation.

3. Teachers can effectively encourage older "refugee" language learners by 1) "eliminating affective barriers," 2) "incorporating adult learning strategies into their teaching," 3) "making the learning situation and the learning materials relevant to the needs and desires of older refugees," 4) "tapping into the goals of the refugee community."

4. Ultimately, Grognet states that the most successful learning programs for elderly refugees are those which incorporate more than just language learning in them. Both Vietnamese and Cambodian refugees have benefited from *new skills* acquired through such

programs (e.g., ability to "initiate emergency calls," ". . . to write their names and addresses and to recognize warning signs on household products").

STRATEGIES AND STRUCTURES

1. By providing a history of the elderly refugees—prior to stating the thesis—Grognet establishes the fact that most Southeast Asian refugees have been through extreme mental and physical trauma prior to ever coming to America, and that the need to acquire another language—English—may not be at the top of everyone's priority list. By offering this short history, the author builds sympathy and encourages an understanding for the newest members in American Society.

2. Before anyone can rationally discuss methods that facilitate adult language learning, one must first identify the sort of obstacles a person is likely to encounter when teaching in anything less than an ideal classroom. Had the author discussed strategies before influential factors, the reader would not have known about limitations and would have assumed everyone was equally teachable.

3. Such journalistic techniques as subheadings and glossed words allow the reader to easily identify the main points of the essay and make rereading or scanning for answers easier. These could be misused, however, in that some readers might only scan the article instead of reading the entire thing, thus missing supporting examples, etc.

4. A call to action is the most appropriate ending for this essay because having given the reader all the necessary information, the author's objective is not merely to inform but to actively involve the reader in becoming part of a program aimed at assisting the elderly refugee. In other words, it doesn't all stop once the pen is put down.

CARLOS BULOSAN

LABOR AND CAPITAL: THE COMING CATASTROPHE

CONTENT

1. The causes of labor exploitation begin first of all with the industrialist who exploits his workers in the name of profit. Powerful industrialists combine together to force the smaller ones out of business. "The bigger the combines they have, the more enormous profits they acquire, which means more exploitation."

2. Economic depression is caused when "the markets are overflowing with surplus." In such instances, Bulosan claims that the only solution that capitalism offers is war.

3. Since ". . . war is not only a slaughter of humanity but also the destruction of culture . . . We must die for peace and not for profit." Students will have a variety of answers as to whether they agree or disagree with Bulosan and why or why not.

4. Even though this was written in 1937, little has changed in the exploitation of employees by large businesses; moreover, we frequently discover instances where companies use unscrupulous means to divest themselves of merchandise. Also, today mergers are often made for the purpose of "quick profit-taking," after which employees are left without jobs or benefits.

STRATEGIES AND STRUCTURES

1. Bulosan refutes the commonly accepted notion that "wars are justified by noble ideals" and claims that instead "wars are fought for profit." Readers' answers will vary on this subject. If students can't decide where they stand on this issue, ask them to consider the Gulf Crisis of 1990–91.

2. Bulosan's topic sentences clearly outline what the essay is about. They are mostly short, simple sentences, but at the same time, they are powerful statements which frame each discussion point supporting the overall thesis of the essay. They also elicit an emotional response from the reader.

3. After reading what Bulosan has to say about the role of the common man in the capitalist system, the only logical way to fight for better living conditions would be through unions. In this sense, the essay builds logically to such a conclusion.

JEANNE WAKATSUKI and JAMES D. HOUSTON

ARRIVAL AT MANZANAR

CONTENT

1. The father has disappeared (arrested) and since the mother does not know what to expect, she moves her family to Terminal Island. The family originally had lived in a white neighborhood, and the children speak only English. When they move to Terminal Island,

Jeanne goes to school with students who speak Japanese, which she does not know. As a result, the students despise her and try to ambush her every day. She also is terrified of "Orientals." The combination of these make her life on Terminal Island a terrible ordeal.

2. According to the author, Terminal Island is a ". . . company town, a ghetto owned and controlled by the canneries." She and her family live in a shack and are surrounded by coarse, vulgar people who ". . . pick on outsiders and persecute anyone who didn't speak as they did."

3. Because the Navy feels it is dangerous to have so many Orientals on Terminal Island, it decides to evacuate Terminal Island because of its proximity to Long Beach Naval Station. As a result of this decision, secondhand dealers prowl the area trying to get the best deals they can from the residents who are forced to sell what they can't take with them. The author's mother is offered only $17.50 for her china, which actually is worth $200. She becomes so angry with this offer that she smashes the china so that the dealer cannot take advantage of her.

4. At first the author is excited about moving to Manzanar because she has never been outside of Los Angeles and has never ridden on a bus. When they arrive at the internment camp, she is still excited and happy and leans out of the window and yells, "Hey! This whole bus is full of Wakatsukis!" Her first impressions are of barbed-wire fences, tents, sand, rows of barracks extending for miles, and people milling around waiting for friends or family to arrive.

5. Answers will vary.

STRATEGIES AND STRUCTURES

1. The author is afraid of other Asian children because of her father's remark that he would sell her to the Chinaman if she didn't behave. She and her family were also the only Orientals who lived in Ocean Park, and she spoke only English. All of these causes lead to the effect of her being terrified during her stay on Terminal Island.

2. The other residents of Terminal Island are roughnecks who speak only a dialect of Japanese peculiar to Kyushu. She shows the effects of being unable to speak the language of the community in such statements as, "They would swagger and pick on outsiders and persecute anyone who didn't speak as they did." She vividly uses examples of their coarse, masculine language to illustrate how the other residents talk and depicts her fear of ambush by saying that she and her brother, ". . . would decide whether to run straight home together, or split up, or try a new and unexpected route."

3. Wakatsuki uses the example of the secondhand dealer and the china set to point out how unfair and frustrating this situation is to the Japanese Americans. Not only has the government decided to intern them illegally, but the general population is profiting from such a move. The only dialogue in this episode appears after the mother begins smashing the china. The secondhand dealer shouts, "Hey! Hey, don't do that! Those are valuable dishes." These words ironically point out the folly of the situation and how the dealer is trying to use the sad situation to line his own pockets.

4. Wakatsuki arranges her material chronologically, strategically using dates to make the entire episode easy to follow. She begins in December of 1941, moves on to February 25, and concludes with the move to Manzanar in early April. Once the family is in the camp, transitional devices such as "After dinner we were taken to Block 16," "The first task was to divide up what space we had," and "That first night in Block 16."

Exposition: Combined Strategies

APPROACHING EXPOSITION

1. After working through the rhetorical modes with students, it may be useful to return to exposition and discuss it as one of the main forms of writing (the others being narration, description, and argumentation). To examine how word choice can often affect the tone in one's essay, it may be worthwhile to initially have students freewrite for an entire class while playing different kinds of music (e.g., jazz, hard rock, classical, country, rap). During the following class session, have students read their compositions aloud to the rest of the class, asking other students to determine *when* there was a change in background music and *how* the author's diction suggested a change to them.

2. To demonstrate that exposition deals with exposing or explaining a topic/issue, select a current scandal in your community and ask students what they know about it. Phrasing your issue as a question may help your students understand just what you wish to uncover or expose. (Since a frequent response may be, "I've been so busy with schoolwork, I haven't had time to watch the news or read the paper for weeks," we suggest you have some handouts you can distribute to the class.)Write the facts—or accusations—on the board as they are presented to you. Finally, relate the activity to the process of expository writing.

DOROTHY PARKER

GOOD SOULS

CONTENT

1. Parker states that "Good Souls" outwardly have no marked peculiarities and that they believe they are just like everyone else; however, certain characteristics do distinguish them from the rest. As children they are always declared "it," theirs is the candy that is always taken away, and they are the ones whom the other children choose to play pranks on. As adults, they are referred to as "meaning well." Good souls rush to our bedsides when we're ill, trying to help but getting in the way. Always trying to help, they insist on taking the worst seats at the theater, always remember birthdays, send cards for every holiday (and even between holidays), visit uninvited, attend only good, wholesome dramas and read only chaste literature. Parker, however, feels that the "most congenial role of the Good Soul is that of advice giver."

2. Parker says there is an impassable barrier between the Good Souls and the rest of the civilized world because even though Good Souls live in "the very thick of the human race, they are forever isolated from it." In fact, the author states that Good Souls are "congenital pariahs." As a result they live their lives, "mingling with the world," but they never really blend in.

3. Parker's tone is quite sarcastic. The reason is that many people probably would consider Good Souls as exemplary citizens, yet Parker views them as pariahs. She tends to address the readers in an informative manner, conveying herself very seriously, which makes us want to take her seriously. She writes about Good Souls logically and chronologically, taking us from their childhood, where they first show signs of being Good Souls, and then showing us how the child is "doomed" to be one all of his or her life, i.e., "Thus does the doomed child go through early youth and adolescence." We further learn that "In health, as in illness, they are always right there, . . ." Through her tone and writing style, we, too, begin to loathe the Good Soul, just as she does.

4. Parker is extremely accomplished at giving concrete and convincing evidence. She never makes a statement without giving one or several examples. For instance, she states that the Good Soul who, "efficiently smooth[es] out your pillow when you have just worked it into the comfortable shape, who creak[s] about the room on noisy tiptoe, who tenderly lay[s] on your fevered brow damp cloths which drip ceaselessly down your neck." If a Good Soul goes away

even for a day, he or she will send postcards to everyone. Above all, Good Souls love to feel the "genial glow of martyrdom—that is all they ask of life."

5. Parker's purpose in defining Good Souls to the point of stereotyping them is to get the reader to see these people exactly as she does. By stereotyping them, she causes us to examine them much more closely. Parker hopes that we will no longer think of them as good people who mean well, but that we will see them as she does—martyrs and possibly bad seeds.

STRATEGIES AND STRUCTURES

1. The most dominant rhetorical strategy at work in this expository essay is example. Parker never once makes a claim without backing it up with one or more of them. Description is another strategy that Parker takes advantage of. By the time the reader has finished this essay, he or she is able to fully "picture" a Good Soul. Persuasion is also in evidence here, since hardly anyone can read this essay without having a different view of a Good Soul.

2. Parker's use of one-sentence paragraphs is an excellent strategical purpose. When all of the other paragraphs are long, the reader's eyes and interest are drawn to these short, but effective, paragraphs. For example, the first one-sentence paragraph comes after two long paragraphs describing these particular people, but she never names them. This name is given in the third paragraph, which simply states, "They are, in short, Good Souls." In no way is she worried about developing any of the ideas contained in these short, one-sentence paragraphs. She already has developed her ideas in preceding paragraphs and uses these short ones to provide emphasis. Another example is in the description of Good Souls as children. She writes a long paragraph describing their activities as youngsters, and then she states, "Mark that child well. He is going to be a Good Soul when he grows up."

3. Parker's ability as a writer is clearly evident in the first paragraph where she immediately grabs the reader's interest by stating, "All about us, living in our families, it may be, there exists a race of curious creatures." Then we are told that these creatures look just like the rest of us. In fact, they are, "built after the popular design; they have the usual number of features, arranged in the conventional manner; . . ." By now, our curiosity is definitely aroused, and we can't wait to learn the identity of these beings. The second paragraph again leads us on, and it isn't until the short, one-sentence paragraph that we learn the identity of them; they are Good Souls.

4. A Good Soul feels impelled to send cards for every occasion. Parker goes so far as to assert that they look for any event in order to send greetings. This is why the author mentions even minor holidays to show that a Good Soul will go to any length to make his presence known. Obviously, Valentine's Day is somewhat important, but Arbor Day and Groundhog Day are definitely minor. Most people will state that companies don't make cards for Arbor and Groundhog Days, but this is more evidence of Parker's sarcasm.

5. Paragraphs 17 through 19 are particularly ironic because Parker takes great pains to meticulously outline what Good Souls appreciate. To this end, she provides readers with a list of over a dozen innocuous names, as if to infer that these people are the guiding lights of goodness, virtue, and social etiquette. However, has any of us ever heard of any of these people? Actually, asking each of your students to take one of the names she mentioned and research them—either on-line or in the library—could be an interesting assignment.

In paragraph 17, Parker notes that the virtues of Good Souls do not lift them "above the enjoyment of popular pastimes;" nonetheless, the people they seem to enjoy (mostly people no one has ever heard of) cause us to suspect that they too are Good Souls. Moreover, we can't help but feel that Good Souls are outsiders instead of representative members of the social, literary, and intellectual community. In paragraph 18, Parker states that "Good Souls, themselves, are no mean humorists." Yet the examples she gives of their humor make us groan rather than make us laugh at true wit, again emphasizing her sarcasm. Finally, by the time Parker mentions that "the most congenial role of the Good Soul is that of the advice giver" in paragraph 19, the reader is almost prepared for an explanation which illustrates the complete opposite. Rather than being impartial counselors, Good Souls offer unsolicited advice. For example, they think it is only right to "point out faults or habits" as well as write letters which state, "'Although you may feel that this is no affair of mine, I think that you really ought to know . . .'"

FRANK LAPEÑA

SHARING TRADITION

CONTENT

1. LaPeña feels that the oral tradition is important in maintaining one's cultural values. Moreover, he contends that the oral tradition has

importance as an art form. Students will have different opinions as to how and why they agree and/or disagree with the author's position.

2. The controlling idea of this essay revolves around the notion that oral tradition must be preserved for the sake of one's culture and to "honor the elders and think of the responsibility that they entrusted to us by sharing tradition with us."

3. Traditionally the elders of any group have passed on information through the oral tradition. Customs and folklore, oftentimes never written down, are available only in this living oral tradition, and if something should happen to the elders alive today, this information would be lost forever.

4. A living oral tradition "accommodates corrections, because the stories are 'known' by the listeners—although today a story could be someone's fantasy and it might be harder to validate."

STRATEGIES AND STRUCTURES

1. LaPeña claims that the oral tradition has a serious impact on how artists visualize "the stories, the characters, the designs and color for art, the atmosphere, and other information which can be useful to an artist." Actually, LaPeña is concerned about deviating from tradition in his own artwork and constantly questions whether something like abstract art is "true to the stories" of his ancestors.

2. LaPeña divides his essay into four major areas, leading to rhetorical questions that he admits he is not able to answer, but, nevertheless, stimulates the reader's interest in the topic and, at the same time, questions his or her place in the oral tradition. The first major problem the author mentions in his essay is that not everyone is capable of being an elder, one who passes on cultural values and beliefs. Furthermore, every time an elder does pass away, it seems he or she leaves a niche that is impossible to fill. The second problem deals with the fact that the young today simply are not certain about how valuable the oral tradition will be in their futures and are not ready to prepare themselves for a role they may never be asked to fulfill. A third obstacle to maintaining the oral tradition resides in the fact that this is not the way modern people learn. Last of all, the future of the oral tradition is in jeopardy because stories are difficult to validate and require a lot of patience to obtain.

3. The topic sentences in "Sharing Tradition" identify the major discussion points of LaPeña's thesis, keeping the reader focused and on track.

CYNTHIA LOPEZ

CURANDERISMO: A HEALING ART

CONTENT

1. Curanderismo, a healing art influenced by the health-care traditions in 16th-century Spain, "uses herbs, ritual prayer, music, dance, and massage to cure people." As Avila explained, curanderismo heals people ". . . by seeking balance in all areas of life: social, physical, and spiritual." In short, curanderismo is a holistic approach to medicine.

2. Lopez's solution to those alienated by modern medicine is to couple the familiar (e.g., the Mexican tradition of folk healing) with the unknown—which can be frightening (modern "scientific" medicine). In doing so, a patient might receive the benefits of both healing methods. It might be worthwhile to point out that there are people who believe in western medicine but could benefit from curanderismo.

3. Avila earned a degree as a registered nurse (RN), was manager of the Psychiatry Department of Thomason General Hospital, and "later became the hospital's director of maternal/child nursing." Avila became the clinical coordinator of the UCLA Neuropsychiatric Institute when she moved to California in 1981.

4. When Avila began her private practice, she specialized in "resolving emotional problems of the adult children of alcoholics, rape survivors, adult incest survivors, and addicts, among others."

5. By understanding and appreciating rather than eschewing or belittling the positive aspects of traditional Mexican medicine, practitioners of Western medicine can demonstrate cultural sensitivity and thereby win the confidence of their Mexican patients. Indeed, as the author pointed out, a "cooperative relationship between healers and physicians" could quite possibly "enhance curanderismo's sometimes bad reputation with the medical establishment."

STRATEGIES AND STRUCTURES

1. Both the first and the last sentences in this essay point out the fact the western medical practices tend to limit what people can do to address their illnesses—medically, spiritually, financially, etc.

2. Lopez wants to establish herself as a credible practitioner of western medicine so that her testimony about curanderismo—which is not textbook material in western medical classrooms—seems to be coming from a knowledgeable, educated individual—capable of looking at things fairly and objectively.

3. Answers will vary a bit for this question. We suggest that you have your students notice the strategic placement of transitional words and phrases, noting how choppy and disunified the essay might seem without them. You should note how Lopez begins by telling her readers about Avila's past, bringing the essay into the present.

4. By expanding her focus from Mexico to all of South America, the author seeks to point to the extent that some form of curanderismo or folk healing exists. She also wishes to demystify the perception of curanderismo as some form of witchcraft. The author highlights yet another point:"The fact remains that for Hispanics, who have always comprised a large part of the uninsured, a visit to the curandero can provide an alternative to no health care at all."

5. This question invites subjective interpretation. You might, however, discuss the way in which Lopez integrates Spanish words harmoniously into her English text parallels her point about the potential harmony between curanderismo (folk medicine) and modern *western* medical practices.

REGINALD LOCKETT

How I Started Writing Poetry

CONTENT

1. The author said he had both pressure and encouragement from his teachers and counselors to begin considering a career after "graduation from high school." He wanted to become a plastic surgeon because "doctors were held in high esteem, particularly in an Afro-American community like West Oakland." Lockett's initial goal was changed when Miss Nettelbeck introduced him to the world of poetry in a creative writing class. She recognized his talent, and he felt pretty good about being "hip to the lip." In time, he "wasn't running down the street with the fellas much anymore." He spent most of his spare moments writing in a manila notebook. Even though his mother was worried he was going to ruin his eyes by reading so much, Lockett kept on "reading and writing, looking forward to Miss Nettlebeck's class twice a week."

2. Lockett loved "history, art, and English." While he had worked his way up "from special education class to college prep courses" by the time he had reached ninth grade, he had "become a full fledged little thug, and had been suspended—and damn near expelled—quite a few times. . . ."Thus, we have the image of a thriving scholar juxtaposed to that of the "budding" street hustler.

3. The author took a serious disliking to Big Martha Dupree who "was known to knock out boys, girls, and teachers when she got the urge." In short, Big Martha was no one to mess with. As Lockett put it: "If Big Martha asked you for a last-day-of-school kiss, you'd better give it up or make an appointment with the dentist."

4. When the author used to "run" with his friends, he stole "clothes, records, liquor, jewelry—anything for the sake of magnifying to the umpteenth degree that image of death-defying manhood" and to prove to himself that he was definitely a "budding Slick Draw Mc-Graw." In contrast, as the essay concludes, the author is stealing books on poets and writers he had come to know through Miss Nettelbeck's creative writing class. No longer a thief in order to prove anything to himself or to maintain an image, the author stole books to feed his insatiable appetite for reading and—by extension—his personal love for writing.

5. While answers to these questions may vary, many students will probably point out that Lockett's audience could be those familiar with street language—the very individuals he grew up with. Another possible audience might be any young "would-be" or "could-be" poet.

STRATEGIES AND STRUCTURES

1. The author spends a good deal of time on providing readers with details about his wild and free lifestyle, his delinquent behavior, and *bad* attitude in order to provide a vivid contrast to the poet he becomes. The important thing here is not only that Lockett became a poet (despite the odds of that ever happening), but also that he gave something up—a way of life that had defined his world for a good part of his life—in order to pursue his career as a poet and a writer.

2. The word choice is extremely informal and colloquial, full of street language. From the start of the essay until its finish, the author's language reflects his street persona which was "going for bad." Though he still says he is as "roguish as ever," his interests have obviously changed as the essay concludes. The fact that his diction remains informal and colloquial is significant; his entire person did not change because he started to appreciate poetry and write it himself. Rather, he used his own voice and made his poetry truly his own.

3. The most obvious rhetorical strategies at work here are narration, description, and informational process analysis.

4. Transitions and linking devices unify the essay and help to maintain coherence as he clearly moves from point-to-point. Of particular importance are "time" transitions. For instance, he begins the essay

with a reference point, "At the age of fourteen," talks more about his delinquency "during" his seventh-grade year, and builds anticipation—keeping the relationship of events in time clear—during the latter paragraphs by beginning each with "when."

5. The topics the author selects to write about are decidedly different and demonstrate the ongoing perplexities of a writer who is divided between poetry he thinks is "safe" to write about—the sea (nature)—and something which he expects to get punished for writing: the poem about the Queen of Drag. The initial poem is more conventional than the latter and is definitely less mature in diction, imagery, and syntax. The latter poem also reflects an authentic voice, for the poem's content was drawn from personal observation. You might have students compare and contrast each poem to determine which poem leaves the poet more vulnerable and why. This may also lead into an interesting dialogue concerning the relationship between a poet's vulnerability and immediacy on one hand, and conventionalism and distance on the other.

WOODY ALLEN
SLANG ORIGINS

CONTENT

1. The purpose of Allen's essay is to provide a guide to some of "the more interesting [slang] origins." One reason Allen may have said he was not interested in slang origins might be to identify himself with a popular audience also disinterested in the topic.

2. In paragraph 3, Allen goes to great lengths to show how "to eat humble pie" originated in the court of Louie the Fat. While the history of the phrase is humorous at times, it is, nonetheless, somewhat credible. In the evolution of a word, mispronunciations of it often determine the form it takes.

3. "Got into a beef," and "to look down one's nose," are slang expressions which, according to Allen, come from marital customs. Both sayings suggest that there has been a lot of tension between the sexes through the ages.

STRATEGIES AND STRUCTURES

1. By beginning and ending the essay with "She's the cat's pajamas," Allen creates a sense of closure, for his discussion of slang origins has come full circle.

2. Allen explains the origin of each slang term chronologically.

3. The humor in Allen's essay is enhanced through his use of absurd explanations, unusual images, and understatement. Allen's uses of humor, poke a little fun at all of us, satirizing the human race and its foibles.

Argumentation:
The Logical Appeal

APPROACHES TO ARGUMENTATION

1. Ask students to get out their thesis notebooks or journals and write
    for ten minutes about a topic or an issue that makes them angry. In-
    sist that they write using vehement words and even profanity if they
    feel so inspired. The objective here is to have students "attack" a
    topic, issue, or person, basing everything they assert on gut-level
    emotions, not substantiated facts. Your ultimate purpose will be to
    show your students how "emotions" may move an audience initially
    but are undoubtedly full of errors in logic which will become appar-
    ent upon close inspection. Therefore, follow up your writing assign-
    ment with a peer activity (e.g., have students critique each other's
    emotional essays) or discuss how to construct a logical essay and
    have students evaluate their own work.

2. Videotape short segments from news programs like *60 Minutes* for
    about a week. Make sure you record people talking about a wide va-
    riety of subjects (e.g., reasons for the present state of U.S. domestic
    policies, the economy, the homeless, etc.). What you really want are
    segments offering information about current social issues, solutions
    to problems, and excuses for not meeting expectations. After you
    play your spliced video to the class, have students evaluate the
    worth of each segment they watched. Now you are ready to tell the
    class how to use inductive and deductive logic to reach verifiable
    conclusions.

BARBARA EHRENREICH

IN DEFENSE OF SPLITTING UP

CONTENT

1. Ehrenreich says that 37% of all American children live with divorced parents, and that "these children already face enough tricky interpersonal situations without having to cope with the public perception that they're damaged goods."

2. Members of the antidivorce movement claim that divorce "may cause teen suicides," create an inability for them to "form lasting attachments," and lead to body mutilation (e.g., piercing the "nipples and nose"). How accurate do your students find the antidivorce movement's causal analysis of a divorce's probable effects on children?

3. Ehrenreich argues that "the real problems for kids will begin when the antidivorce movement starts getting its way because "the more militant among the members want to 're-stigmatize' divorce with the cultural equivalent of a scarlet D." If anything, people should work to "de-stigmatize" divorce because children from broken homes already have enough social pressures working against their health, growth and development.

4. Money—*the root of all evil*—seems to be the primary motivation behind the philosophy of the antidivorce movement. Beginning with the opening paragraph, Ehrenreich observes that cuts in social programs that help all United States citizens—including children of single-parent families—do not bother the public as a whole, yet disingenuous tears begins to flow at the mention of divorce. The psychological, emotional, and even physical costs of growing up as a child of a bad marriage seem like insignificant details as far as the antidivorce movement is concerned.

5. Answers will vary here, but many students will probably agree that the way out of the poverty experienced by many single-parent families, especially mothers, would be to "toughen child-support collection and strengthen the safety net of supportive services for low-income families—including childcare, Medicaid, and welfare."

STRATEGIES AND STRUCTURES

1. Ehrenreich begins her essay by stating the problem with the current antidivorce movement, and she focuses the controlling ideas for her entire essay with the first sentence of the second paragraph: "But if divorce itself hasn't reduced Americans to emotional cripples, then

the efforts to restrict it undoubtedly will."(You might take this opportunity to remind readers that, although the thesis statement usually falls in the introductory paragraph, there are exceptions to the general rule.) Ehrenreich goes on to argue how and why the proposed restrictions on divorce could be more damaging than nurturing for children and concludes that "grownups have to do difficult and costly things, whether they like doing them or not."

2. "In Defense of Splitting Up," the title of Ehrenreich's essay, establishes her position on the topic of divorce. She notes that "the growing antidivorce movement is blinded to the costs of bad marriages," and essentially, that the institution of divorce is oftentimes more defensible than an unhealthy relationship between parents.

3. Ehrenreich establishes her credibility as a fair critic of the antidivorce movement by acknowledging the group's claim that the divorce rate in the United States did rise following the "no-fault divorce laws." However, she quickly points out that the "divorce rate was already rising at a healthy clip *before* that, so there's no guarantee that the repeal of no-fault divorce laws will reduce the divorce rate now. The rhetoric of the antidivorce movement does not provide specific representative evidence that validates its argument but relies on half truths and fallacious logic—most notably the *post hoc ergo propter hoc* fallacy. The antidivorce movement also bases its conclusions on faulty or stilted statistics, thereby committing the fallacy of *faulty sampling*. Where, for instance, are the numerous childless couples in the antidivorce movement's statistics? For such couples, what would be the purpose of remaining in an unhappy, dysfunctional union?

4. In a "good divorce," both parents remain equally committed to the "financial and emotional responsibility for the kids." Thus, rather than try to hold together a dysfunctional relationship between parents that could be harmful to all parties concerned, perhaps "the reformers should concentrate on improving the *quality* of divorce—by, for example, requiring prenuptial agreements specifying how the children will be cared for in the event of a split."

You might have your students update some of the details suggested in Ehrenreich's essay—such as what states are attempting to enforce measures to make it more difficult to get divorced—by asking them to research the issue on the Internet. Starting on June 1, 1997, for instance (more than a year after Ehrenreich published her essay in *Time*), Judge James Sheridan of Lenawee County, Michigan, stated that people who want to get married through clergy, a magistrate, a judge, or a mayor must first attend "marriage education classes." As stated in *USA Today* on April 10, 1997, "Enthusiasm for requiring premarital counseling as a way to reduce the divorce rate is not limited to the Wolverine State. The move is under discussion in at least nine others: Arizona, Illinois, Iowa, Maryland, Minnesota, Mississippi, Missouri, Oregon, and Washington.

PAULA GUNN ALLEN

WHO IS YOUR MOTHER?
RED ROOTS OF WHITE FEMINISM

CONTENT

1. Laguna tribe members identify themselves through their mothers. A person is able to derive a great benefit from this because ". . . your mother's identity is the key to your own identity."

2. Not knowing your mother is a great disadvantage; it is the same as being lost, for it is ". . . failure to remember your significance, your reality, your right relationship to earth and society."

3. Contemporary Americans have not held on to their cultural origins. Most immigrants are eager to begin a new life and throw away all of their cultural ties, ". . . often seeing their antecedents as backward, restrictive, even shameful." American institutions such as the government, churches, and the corporate system also advocate giving up any connection to native traditions.

4. If contemporary American culture were to adopt the traditional views of Native Americans, women would have a more important role, goods would be distributed more equally, senior citizens would be more respected, our natural resources would be more protected, and we could do away with war.

5. Native Americans believe in remembering and preserving their customs, value the individual, and consider women important while the Americans do not. In the contemporary American way of life, customs are not important and women and the individual are not valued, which the Native American believes leads to a loss of identity and oppression. Just the opposite is true in the Native American culture where customs and traditions are important, and there is a strong sense of identity and self-worth.

STRATEGIES AND STRUCTURES

1. Allen begins by asking the question: "Who is your mother?" and states that this is important in the Laguna Pueblo. By asking this

question, she has immediately gotten the attention of her readers, who more than likely belong to a society that values men above women.

2. Allen's thesis is presented in the introductory paragraph where she states, "But naming your own mother (or her equivalent) enables people to place you precisely within the universal web of your life, in each of its dimensions: cultural, spiritual, personal, and historical." By showing that the naming of a person's mother is connected to the cultural, spiritual, personal, and historical facets of one's life, the reader is able to see how each contributes to a person's sense of worth.

3. Throughout this essay, Allen continually compares and contrasts the lifestyles of Native Americans and Americans to illustrate that Native Americans have the better of the two cultures. In the conclusion she shows how the adoption of Native American ways will bring about self-respect, a safer environment, and even peace.

4. By presenting all of the benefits adoption of Native American customs can bring about in the conclusion, Allen has skillfully led the reader through her argument to the point where he or she can understand and accept these benefits.

IMAMU AMIRI BARAKA

SOUL FOOD

CONTENT

1. Baraka's argument of fact is that African Americans—contrary to what some may believe—have a language and characteristic cuisine unique to their culture.

2. Making extensive use of illustration and example, Baraka vividly and convincingly argues his thesis.

3. "Uptown" in this essay refers either to the part of town away from the main business district or the middle of the city. While not a word used exclusively by African Americans, students may have a wide range of responses to the second part of this question. Comparing student responses—and the basis of their reasoning—could prove a fruitful classroom activity.

4. With so much available in the way of excellent African American food, only a "square" or naive person (e.g., the author who claimed African Americans had no language or cuisine) would bother eating at Nedicks.

STRATEGIES AND STRUCTURES

1. Baraka uses the African American terms for food first in order to identify their cultural origins. Then he defines the food that may be unfamiliar to a lot of people. There does seem to be a two-part argument here because most Americans never have tasted "soul food," and Baraka is attempting to convince them to give up their quick-frozen, bland diets and try something different and delicious.

2. The use of slang terms in this essay enables Baraka to show, rather than just tell his readers, that African Americans have a unique vocabulary (language), thereby arguing—once again—through illustration and example. (How could anyone challenge his argument of fact after so many examples?)

3. While Baraka focuses his attention on food throughout the essay—which is only appropriate since he is arguing that African Americans have a cuisine of their own—he incorporates African American dialect into his argument. Doing so helps him to disprove the notion that African Americans do not have a unique language/dialect.

JUDY CHRISTRUP

THIS LAND WAS YOUR LAND

CONTENT

1. Vanishing jobs in the timber industry are caused by ". . . mill efficiency, mill automation and exports . . ." Thus, neither the spotted owl nor any other animal is to blame for the loss of jobs in timber-related industries. The spotted owl is just an emotional distraction presented to an unaware public to divert attention away from the real issues behind decreasing employment of U.S. citizens in logging.

2. *Record profits* in the logging industry motivate timber companies to "clear-cut" their lands, thereby creating a *logging crisis.*

3. The Forestry Service makes Forest Service land available to logging companies and is rewarded by selling standing timber. However, as Christrup points out, over two-thirds of our national forests lose money on the sales. The irony here is that "American taxpayers are actually subsidizing the cutting of our national forests."

4. Some of the groups or organizations which oppose the cutting of old forests include: The Sierra Club, The Wilderness Society, Earth First, and the Ancient Forest Alliance. There also are special "grass roots groups," such as: Protect our Woods, Western North Carolina Alliance, Mark Twain Forest Watchers, and Regional Association of Concerned Environmentalists (RACE), who oppose the cutting of second- and third-growth national forests. While some of the older, more established groups tend to be more conservative, the newer groups are becoming more militant, engaging in such activities as blockading logging roads and moving into the designated cutting areas to hassle "the cutters to distraction."

STRATEGIES AND STRUCTURES

1. The verb "was," which indicates past tense, immediately creates tension and a sense of foreboding because it implies something—ownership—has been lost.

2. The author appeals to everyone—especially those who "buy into" the idea that the protection of the spotted owl is to blame for job shortages in the timber industry. The author begins by stating the problem: that only 5 percent of the virgin forests remains, and that some citizens are trying to stop the cutting of virgin trees while others side with the timber industry. Then, with the use of statistics, she shows the negative results of unchecked cutting and how the industry and the Forest Service are helping each other while the taxpayer subsidizes the cutting. She ends the article by offering solutions, stating what environmentalist groups are proposing to end the cutting.

3. Within the first two sentences of this essay, the author clearly points out how logging has decimated "old growth forests." The final sentence in the introductory paragraph ". . . the Pacific Northwest is hosting a showdown of sorts for the campaign to save the last shreds of ancient forest," is the controlling idea of the essay.

4. Answers will vary although the fact that Christrup gives exact statistics is much more convincing than emotional appeals.

5. Christrup makes her call to action in paragraph 13. This is a logical place for it because the author has had time to 1) present her argument of fact, and 2) based upon the facts, the need to act seems ethical and reasonable. Placing this "call to action" earlier in the essay would not have been as convincing to the reader, since she would not have identified the problem requiring the action.

MARK CHARLES FISSEL

Distance Learning and American Society

CONTENT

1. In his opening paragraph, Fissel states that "video's potential to educate has not yet been fully understood or realized," and he goes on to argue that interactive video instruction—distance learning—transmits ". . . benefits to those in America who have not had ready access to higher education."

2. Distance learning "brings school to the students." They keep in touch with the teacher through "teleconferencing" and take periodic examinations over the semester which are "proctored by site supervisors."

3. Individuals who cannot—or choose not—to attend college in a traditional classroom setting benefit the most from distance learning.

4. According to Fissel, most professional fields, white- and blue-collar jobs alike, have something to gain from interactive video instruction. The constant inservice training, especially for those in the areas of health care and technology, provided by video instruction is not only cost-effective but convenient for the students.

5. While Fissel notes that television has the tendency to "homogenize" culture and threaten "cultural diversity," he also argues that video instruction can enable one to strengthen his or her identity within a social community (e.g., Native American and religious groups). Therefore, video instruction has the "potential to preserve and accommodate cultures as well as 'standardize' them."

STRATEGIES AND STRUCTURES

1. By presenting the thesis in the first paragraph, the major argument at hand (video instruction offers learning opportunities for those who formerly did not have a "ready access to higher education") becomes firmly established in the reader's mind prior to any essay development.

2. Using the five journalistic questions (who, what, when, where, why), Fissel anticipates reader inquiries and attempts to answer them within his text. Anticipating and responding to potential reader questions (possibly translated into objections like, "Yes, but . . . !") strengthens the logical and ethical appeal of an argument.

3. Each of the body paragraphs in Fissel's essay begins with a topic sentence or a rhetorical question followed by a definitive topic sentence. Such sentences guide his paragraph development.

4. Fissel develops each section of his essay using specific concrete references and examples. For instance, he illustrates who benefits from distance learning, mentioning hospital and corporate workers, military personnel, and prisoners.

5. The author uses outside sources—authoritative testimony—to substantiate what he says. Among other things, referring to outside sources suggests the author is well read on his subject. This in turn enhances the credibility of his claims. (Student opinions may vary regarding the effectiveness of using outside sources.)

DOUGLAS LAYCOCK
PEYOTE, WINE, AND THE FIRST AMENDMENT
CONTENT

1. Laycock's concern is that government could interfere with our constitutional rights if the Oregon Supreme Court were to limit the use of peyote in supervised worship ceremonies. His fear is that government could eventually limit other religious freedoms which would go against the First Amendment that guarantees the free exercise of religion.

2. Answers to this question will vary as to whether or not Smith and Black's supervisor treated them fairly. Students, however, should take into consideration: 1) the First Amendment, 2) the agency's rule against drug or alcohol use, 3) the fact that there is no evidence that Christians or Jews had been discharged for the use of wine in their religious rituals, 4) Smith and Black's discrimination charge against the agency, and finally, 5) the agency's action of paying some of their lost salaries while not admitting to discrimination.

3. The author points out that the peyote ritual is similar to communion in the Christian religion since the wine is central to the ceremony just as peyote is in the ritual practiced by the Native Americans. Also, Christians adore and hold the wine in reverence since they believe the deity is present in it. Christians, however, do not become intoxicated at communion. In the Jewish ceremony Purim, the participant is taught to celebrate it by getting drunk. The peyote ritual is different because the participant sees God due to the mind-altering effects of the drug, which is not a part of any Christian or Jewish traditions.

4. Answers may vary to this question, but it is ironic that alcohol, one of the chief contributors to the deaths of Native Americans, was allowed for religious purposes during prohibition, and today only 23

states allow the religious use of peyote, a drug that has been used by the Native Americans for at least 400 years and is not a major cause of death among Native Americans.

5. The reader knows Laycock is not advocating the use of peyote for a high when he states that it is, ". . . no modern innovation designed to evade the drug laws." Also, his major argument is not about peyote; it is to educate the reader as to how easy it would be for the government to take away his or her freedom to worship.

STRATEGIES AND STRUCTURES

1. The author points out that peyote is used by a minor religious group, and prohibiting its usage would affect only a small number of people; however, the First Amendment guarantees religious freedom, and interfering with the rights of only a few eventually could lead to tampering with the rights of us all.

2. The separation of church and state is an essential part of this since it is this separation that protects every person's right to practice the religion that he or she believes in. If this separation were not guaranteed, the government could tell all of us how to worship.

3. Laycock points out that peyote is sacramental and the object of worship since it is used to enable the participant to experience God directly, and *it is a sacrilege to use it for nonreligious purposes.* The author's argument is more logical because he compares and contrasts the use of peyote with Christian and Jewish rituals involving wine, pointing out the Christians have a ". . . reverence and even adoration for the consecrated wine and the belief that the deity is present in the wine."

4. To warn the reader that Americans do not have true freedom to worship as they choose, Laycock shows how Smith and Black are discriminated against by their employer, the Oregon courts, and the Supreme Court. The employer wants Smith and Black to agree not to ask for job reinstatement because of the delicate nature of this case, especially since the company has not answered the discrimination charge made by the two of them while paying some of their lost salaries. If the two had filed a suit to be reinstated and the company had refused, a very strong case could be brought against the company, a case Smith and Black could possibly win. The Supreme Court made no judgment in this case and sent it back to Oregon's state courts, asking, ". . . whether Oregon would recognize a religious exception to its criminal laws against possession or consumption of peyote." This was a smart move by the Supreme Court because the Oregon courts decided that prosecuting Smith and

Black would violate the federal Constitution. The author wants us to conclude that all of us could have our religious freedoms in jeopardy had Oregon been allowed to prosecute Smith and Black. Answers will vary as to why this strategy does or does not work.

5. Laycock wants us to feel uncomfortable with the government and judges deciding which religions and religious festivals are important and which are not because then, "The government could acquire a *de facto* power to review theology and liturgy."These bans could ultimately lead to the end of our religious freedoms.

6. Answers to these questions will vary. (You might want students to explain their deductive reasoning as part of the assignment and relate it back to argumentative essays.)

12

Persuasion: The Emotional Appeal

APPROACHES TO PERSUASION

1. Many writers use emotionally charged words when writing persuasive essays. In order to help students see the emotion contained in certain words, list three or four emotionally charged words on the board and have them cluster the emotions they feel for each word. (You may want to model this activity first and/or create a list of emotions: fear, hate, love, joy, etc.) Next, have students share their clusters with other students, explaining why they had particular emotional responses. Finally, put a topic on the board and, as a class, brainstorm all the emotionally charged words associated with it. Of course, you'll want to discuss the abuses of the emotional appeal and emotionally charged words.

2. Introduce students to *ethos, pathos, and logos*—three different kinds of appeals used in persuasion—through a visual medium before turning to the analysis and production of words. First, find and cut out ads from magazines, such as *Time* and *Newsweek,* for all three appeals. In small groups, where each student has located examples of each of the appeals, have them identify and then discuss why the various approaches to persuasion work. (What assumptions is the advertiser making about his or her audience? What was particularly convincing about the ad?) Finally have groups make a class presentation, showing the ads from the magazines to the rest of the class, identifying and explaining the appeals used, and then presenting and discussing their own ideas for advertising their own product.

GORE VIDAL

DRUGS

CONTENT

1. Vidal states that to stop drug addiction in a short time all drugs should be made available to the public, provided at cost and labeled with a precise description of what effect each drug will have on the user. Answers will vary as to whether his argument is convincing or weak.

2. There is a parallel between the government's attempt to do away with drugs and its previous attempt to enforce prohibition. When alcohol was forbidden, the greatest crime wave in history took place, thousands of deaths resulted from bad alcohol, and people had contempt for the law. We see the same effects today; there is also another crime wave of gigantic proportions, a great number of deaths have been reported from overdosing on bad drugs, and again there is an obvious contempt for the law.

3. Vidal persuades us well that the American moralist lives in a time vacuum by showing us that even though we have made almost the same mistake as we did during prohibition, our memories don't go back that far. The government is attempting the same solution twice and thus is making the same mistake twice.

4. Responses will vary here. However, this question could provide a valuable opportunity to discuss how sexist and/or racist language alienates one's audience.

STRATEGIES AND STRUCTURES

1. Vidal's logic is evident in the comparison of prohibition with what is happening in drug legislation today. He also shows how drugs keep the Mafia and the Bureau of Narcotics in business. Emotional appeal is seen when he points out how kids got hooked on heroin, and death dramatically increased when marijuana importation was curtailed.

2. Answers will vary as to how well the author addresses individual concerns regarding drug abuse. Vidal shows us why drug abuse exists but goes on to report that it will not go away because of America's devotion "to the idea of sin and its punishment." He considers the side of the drug dealer and the drug enforcer. He does not, however, consider the side of the drug user.

3. The author first asks if anything sensible will be done to end the drug problem and then answers by saying "Of course not." The effect of this is demoralizing and depressing. At first, this answer appears to be contrary to his thesis, "It is possible to stop most drug addiction in the United States within a very short time." However, making drugs available at a cheap price does not go along with the public's and the government's way of thinking. He concludes by pointing out that not only is selling drugs a big business, but fighting drug addiction is almost as big. As Vidal states, ". . . the combination of sin and money is irresistible . . . the situation will only grow worse."

4. The author is an authority since he has tried every drug once—even though he liked none of them. Had he not sampled the drugs, his argument would have been much less persuasive.

PHYLLIS McGINLEY

WOMEN ARE BETTER DRIVERS

CONTENT

1. Although the essay does not have a single thesis statement, her controlling idea is initially presented to the reader with the essay title: "Women Are Better Drivers." Then, after a tongue-in-cheek discussion about the relative merits and accomplishments of men, she modestly notes that there are only two things where women excel: having babies (the end of paragraph 1) and driving (a single sentence for paragraph 2). Obviously, no one can refute her initial claim that women are better at having babies than men, so she need not argue the issue (her first argument has already been won!). It is her second point which she needs to support in order to make believers out of her readers.

2. Men can "mend the plumbing, cook, invent atomic bombs, design the Empire waistline, and run the four-minute mile." References to inventing "atomic bombs" and designing such things as the "Empire waistline" are questionable achievements, of course, which is the very reason she incorporates them into her list. Subsequent male abilities like being able to throw a ball overhand and growing a beard are also rather minute or insignificant accomplishments.

3. The author reasons that women are better drivers than men because: (1) *they receive the most practice.* Indeed, she claims that outside of taxi cab drivers and truck drivers, women are the ones who "really handle the cars of the nation." Then McGinley supports

her claim with references to the daily chores like shopping, ferrying their husbands," and "driving their young to school and dentists and dancing classes and scouting meetings." (You might point out how McGinley strung together several "ands" to emphasize the unending nature of their task of driving. (2) *Men lack caution and are prone to distraction* when they drive. In part this is because men feel a need to show off—or not be "shown-up by another driver." Women are practical when it comes to driving; men are not. The author uses a lot of personal testimony—tales of her husband's driving—and shows that he "becomes a tyrant behind a wheel." (3) *Women are more reasonable than men.* They have the good sense to ask for advice if they "don't know their routes exactly." Women also take down directions whereas impatient men just say, ". . . oh never mind, I'll look it up on the map."

4. An automobile is like a "shining chariot" to a man, implying that his car is an object for him to love like "the lone ranger loves his horse." As such, a man feels honor for his automobile and "No one must out-weave or out-race him."

5. Simon Legree was a slave dealer and hideous villain in Harriet Beecher Stowe's novel, *Uncle Tom's Cabin.* His brutal nature is easy to equate with the monster men turn into once they get behind the wheel of a car. In short, the author uses the simile "like Simon Legree" to characterize male drivers physically and mentally.

6. McGinley says women are used to advice from their "mother, teachers, beaus, husbands, and eventually their children." As a result, asking and accepting advice on how to get somewhere by car is second nature for a woman; it simply makes sense. Men, in contrast, hate to take and often don't listen to advice when they receive it.

STRATEGIES AND STRUCTURES

1. The author contrasts her "practical" concern about luggage and wardrobe to her husbands, and eventually their children." As a result, asking and accepting advice on how to get somewhere by car is second nature for a woman; it simply makes sense. Men, in contrast, hate to take and often don't listen to advice when they receive it.

2. McGinley attempts to persuade her readers by providing them with contrasts which show how women drive in a *positive light* and how men drive in a *dark shadow.* Some of these contrasts include: (1) Women are cautious and men are reckless on the road; (2) Women practice driving five days a week whereas men receive their practice on weekends (the reference to innings and outings suggest where they drive, and, possibly the condition they are in when they drive

home—*drunk*); (3) Women have a healthy attitude about driving since they recognize the automobile for what it is—a mode of transportation; men have an unhealthy attitude towards driving because they see it as a way to show off, to demonstrate their manliness; (4) Women are practical about planning road trips and appreciating them, but men are only concerned with their maps. That is not to say that maps are unimportant, but McGinley's husband, for instance, is obsessed by the squiggly lines he drew to the exclusion of everything else around him. Interestingly, in paragraph 4 McGinley makes an appeal to authority. The State of New York seems to fully endorse her thesis; there, insurance policies are more expensive for men than for women because the latter are better drivers.

3. McGinley's humorous tone definitely helps her to argue an issue that is difficult to empirically prove. True, insurance policies are more expensive for men than women, so what she says early on in the essay is verifiable. However, for the better part of her essay, since she is using *values* as the criteria for determining that women are better drivers than men—and values tend to be somewhat subjective—her lighthearted tone is probably the best strategical approach to her topic. By poking fun at the inability of men to meet her standards or her set of values, she seeks to persuade a reader emotionally and ethically. Student answers to the last part of this question will vary.

4. The inclusion of dialogue makes the dynamics between male and female drivers seem *real*. The dialogue tends to draw on truisms or statements we have heard many times from both sexes. Good examples of this are the "tag questions" offered by McGinley, herself: "Shouldn't we stop here?" (paragraph 9), and "Isn't that the City of Gold?" (paragraph 17). Other examples might be the responses for the irritated male driver: "Who's driving?" (paragraph 10), and "What does the map say?" (paragraph 17). Such dialogue is representative—though certainly not exclusive or definitive—of both sexes by virtue of the fact that one has probably heard women and men ask comparable questions or make similar comments.

5. While the author would comment on the "pretty stars" and the "City of Gold" as they approached the *Pearly Gates,* her husband would still have tunnel vision, be a reckless driver, and maintain his obsession with the superficial (no appreciation of nature and aesthetic beauty at all). As she says in the final paragraph, her husband would respond to anything she asked or pointed out to him by snapping, "Never mind your golden cities . . . as he nearly collides with a meteor. . . . Just keep your eye on the map."

   This essay was originally published in 1959, but the argument about who are better drivers, women or men, persists. You might have your students do an update of McGinley's article.

MICHAEL DORRIS

FETAL ALCOHOL SYNDROME

CONTENT

1. This essay focuses on the dangers of "prenatal alcohol use" and by extension drug use (see paragraph 5).

2. Prenatal alcohol abuse by women damages their infants' motor development: "Year-old children of women who had one or more drinks a day score lower on psychomotor tests than children whose mothers had less than one drink a day."

3. At the time this article was written in March 1990, there was only "one residential treatment program (Odyssey House) for pregnant women . . ." in New York.

4. Alaska has the highest percentage of fetal alcohol syndrome.

5. Dorris points out that "illegal drugs, such as crack cocaine" also tend to impair babies at birth. Your students may want to elaborate on other types of illegal drugs that harm children. The author believes such births are on the increase because of inadequate treatment facilities and inadequate prenatal care. For example, he notes only one facility exists in New York and that "16% of all American women who gave birth have had inadequate prenatal care."

STRATEGIES AND STRUCTURES

1. Statistics focus readers on verifiable data and expose information in a logical fashion.

2. Dorris's appeal to authority shows that he is not talking "off the top of his head." He uses the information provided by specific authorities to back his persuasive argument. The consequences of pregnant mothers' drinking is dramatic and frightening. However, rather than explore fetal alcohol syndrome from the point view of an emotional, outraged individual, he logically approaches the subject. Still, the indignation and emotion behind the piece is ever-present—just not overpowering.

3. Dorris's use of transitional words and phrases are most noticeable at the beginning of paragraphs and clearly establish a sense of time and place, thereby strengthening coherence. Some examples include: "Since the publication of this book . . ." (Paragraph 1); "On January 11, 1990 . . ." (Paragraph 2); "With less of the enzyme that breaks down alcohol . . ." (Paragraph 3); "Meanwhile . . ." (Paragraph 5); finally, "Although the legislatures of Arizona, Illinois, Minnesota, Oregon, Pennsylvania, New Hampshire and Florida . . ." (Paragraph 8).

4. Dorris's essay attempts to persuade the reader of the seriousness and pervasiveness of FAS by providing facts that support his main idea. This naturally leads to a call for action in the concluding paragraph for "more effort in funding" by society. By convincing the reader of the seriousness of FAS, Dorris has set the reader up for a call to action to deal with this problem.

5. Although answers to this question may vary a bit, one thing can be said for certain: state and federal governments have not addressed the needs of alcoholic and drug-abusing mothers. Society needs to become aware of the problem and to fund treatment centers and adequate prenatal care.

RON GLASS

RACISM AND MILITARISM: THE NUCLEAR CONNECTION

CONTENT

1. Glass presents his thesis in the first sentence which states, "The nuclear industry, in alliance with major U.S. corporations, has blatantly disregarded and disrespected people of color in the search for profits."

2. The government and corporations need uranium ore (a radioactive material) to create nuclear weapons, and this is found in the Western United States, Canada, Australia, and South Africa. Seventy-two percent of the resources are found on lands belonging to native people, i.e., Native Americans, Aborigines, etc. The problem presented by this fact is that most of these natives have treaties, and if the governments honor these treaties, no uranium will be mined.

3. When uranium is mined nearby, Native Americans and others face health hazards such as: contaminated water and air, a cancer risk 100 percent greater than the general population, genetic diseases, such as ". . . club foot, subluxated hips, mental retardation, diabetes, heart disease, rheumatic fever, sterility, and cancers."

4. Additional problems faced by Native Americans are: their homes, schools, and playgrounds are made of radioactive materials, food is grown on contaminated land, and some are exposed to radioactivity. The biggest problem is that the government does nothing to stop or rectify these injustices.

STRATEGIES AND STRUCTURES

1. Glass immediately presents his thesis to shock the reader and also as a portent of more shocking statistics to come.

2. The author presents his argument in a foolproof way, by presenting one shocking statement after another, backed up by statistics, scientific data, and historical events which add validity to his statements. Answers will vary as to whether his use of such data is effective.

3. Glass's use of many statistics is to convert the reader to his way of thinking. Most of his statistics are shocking, which help to convince any reader who is not on his side.

4. The author presents many more problems faced by Native Americans exposed to nuclear dangers in one paragraph because all of the evidence prior to this paragraph has given reasons for these dangers, and the reader is now prepared to accept the statistics without further asking why. Only short explanations are necessary, such as, "These additional problems are related to socioeconomic status, population size, and relationship to the land and food supplies." Glass uses such linking words as: *additionally, also,* and *finally.*

KIM STANLEY ROBINSON

A COLONY IN THE SKY

CONTENT

1. To terraform a planet's surface simply means to change it until "Earth's life forms can survive there." Robinson admits that the hypothesis for terraforming a planet's surface is rooted in tales of science fiction.

2. To make Mars inhabitable for earthly life forms, one would have to "add nitrogen and oxygen to the atmosphere; pump water to the surface; cook for decades, spicing first with cynabacteria, then with all the rest of the earth's plants and animals, adding them in the order they evolved" on earth. Unlike the United States' goal to put a person on the Moon after a decade of space exploration in the 1960s, the recipe for terraforming Mars would take at least 300 years—hardly the sort of short project current scientists and politicians will witness in their lifetime.

3. Robinson claims that most of the reasons for space exploration and a "crossing to Mars" will be for the sake of better knowledge of the universe. This would include verifying if there really are "fossil

bacteria" on the planet—something the scientific community recently claimed is a high probability after studying a meteor from Mars which landed in Antarctica. He also admits that some people may have reasons for traveling to Mars—like looking for Elvis. Here he indicates that *not* all people want to think about Mars and use it as "a research site to sharpen Earth management skills."

4. Robinson claims that several people will land on Mars in the 21st century, and that even though many will take a base or "space station" on Mars for granted in a very short time, "something very big will have begun." The rest of the essay goes on to argue how and why "something big will have begun," following the first step towards the colonization of the planet: research.

5. Answers will vary for this question.

STRATEGIES AND STRUCTURES

1. The first and last paragraphs in "A Colony in the Sky" provide readers with a framing device for the entire essay: space exploration and its meaning for the human race. The issue of "probabilities" underline the controlling idea in both paragraphs. That is, in the introductory paragraph. Robinson asserts that it is quite probable that "one day early next century, several people will land on Mars." In the concluding paragraph, Robinson states that "here on Earth in the age of the quarterly statement," it is equally as probable people may spoil the pristine "red planet." Thus, what humanity really needs is to "work out a sustainable way of life on Earth." That way, a voyage to Mars and its colonization would be a positive environmental project—instead of the answer to the ecological mismanagement and pollution found on planet Earth.

2. This question invites diverse student responses, and it may be well worthwhile to spend some class time brainstorming the multiple possibilities inferred by the phrase "something big." (Indeed, Robinson, himself, does not seem totally convinced the event recognized as "something big" will be positive in nature—but it will be dynamic!) Generally, Robinson argues that reaching Mars represents one goal but making the planet like Earth is another. On one hand, Robinson seems to like the idea of a colony on Mars. On the other hand, he also recognizes and hints at the ever present dangers of human colonization. In paragraph 7, for instance, he states "Many larger species are in danger of extinction from us" because "we have rearranged much of the land [on Earth], and we have altered the atmosphere to the point where the global climate in the future will be a matter of legislation and industrial practice." Obviously, such

facts are hardly compelling reasons for altering the nature of a
planet in order to make it a hospitable habitat for members of a
"throw-away" society. Quite the contrary! If anything, Robinson implies that people must temper their adventurous spirit with caution.
He then concludes that it is a "good thing occasionally to contem-
plate a really long-term project."

3. Logic, ethics, and emotions appeal to readers throughout Robinson's
    essay. Based upon past space projects and present space stations,
    Robinson reasons that Americans will land on Mars. Ironically,
    Robinson logically and ethically reasons that we must explore Mars
    and alter its biosphere for earthly habitation because the human
    race, through its lack of vision and immediate concern, has de-
    stroyed many forms of flora and fauna. Furthermore, he notes that
    the future of even more species of plants and animals is in jeopardy
    and faces almost certain extinction unless "we protect them from
    us." Robinson does seem to suggest, however, that scientific explo-
    ration, grounded in emotions along the lines of explorer bravado
    and conquest exhilaration, people frequently supersede rational
    thinking when it comes to space travel and galactic colonization.

4. Students might first consider the audience for whom Robinson
    writes before drawing any conclusions about his "recipe" metaphor.
    "A Colony in the Sky" appeared in the September 23, 1996, edition
    of *Newsweek,* a magazine written and edited in order to relate to
    the masses, not an elitist group (e.g., *Omni,* a magazine which tar-
    gets people with exceptionally high I.Q.s). If Robinson had ex-
    plained terraforming only from a scientific perspective, full of
    jargon and concepts foreign to the majority of his audience, his
    essay would lack accessibility. Granted, the "recipe" metaphor makes
    the complex process of terraforming seem almost too simple, but
    one must remember that his essay's objective is to inform and per-
    suade the general public—not the critical scientific community—
    with his views on colonizing Mars.

5. The use of occasional scientific diction throughout this essay re-
    minds readers of the serious nature of Robinson's subject without
    confusing them with dense nomenclature. The scientific diction he
    uses has helped establish his credibility as an authority on his sub-
    ject. Have your students go through this essay and gloss every scien-
    tific word or words carrying scientific connotations. Then have
    them write a simple synonym for each. You might also have stu-
    dents state their responses to the second Language and Vocabulary
    question and discuss how the synonyms they found for scientific
    words would or would not strengthen the sense or appeal of Robin-
    son's essay.

NORTH CHINESE/VIETNAMESE ELDER

I WANT TO LIVE WITHOUT TROUBLE
AS TOLD TO JAMES M. FREEMAN

CONTENT

1. The author *himself* has always been a stranger. He lived in Vietnam but was considered a foreigner. The same is true when he moved to America. Most people, therefore, have been strangers to him. The Communists treated him badly and now that he is living in the U.S., he finds most Americans are selfish and too individualistic. This fear and distrust he has felt all his life cause him to look at things in a different light. As a result, he thinks that Americans have too much freedom, one of the main themes of this essay.

2. The author believes that a society with too much freedom breeds citizens who care only about themselves and not the common good. Thus, in caring only for themselves, they have become careless and inconsiderate.

3. There are parallels between the author's life in Vietnam and the life he is living in the U.S. During the French rule in Vietnam, the Chinese were set apart from other Vietnamese. When the Communists took over, at first Chinese were treated well, but later, when war developed between China and Vietnam, they were asked to leave. This action caused the author to distrust "strangers." He has been set apart for so much of his life that it is no wonder he looks for the negative side of American life. In examining the citizens of the U.S., he sees such perils as too much freedom, lack of patriotism, and too great an emphasis on capitalism.

4. In the author's opinion, too much individualism makes people extremely self-centered. When they think only of themselves, they do not care for other people, the common good, and, particularly, their country. Patriotism then becomes nonexistent and ". . . people can sell secrets to the Russians just for money, for profits." As a result, individualism and selfishness have led to the love of profit, which causes people, for example, to ignore the safety of others in order to earn higher profits.

STRATEGIES AND STRUCTURES

1. The author began his life as a "foreigner" in Vietnam. When he emigrated to the U.S., he again was a foreigner. Because he has spent his life being an outsider, he has a different view of the countries he has lived in; therefore, he does not see America as most citizens do.

2. The author concludes on an optimistic note because he has noticed some positive aspects about the U.S. and its citizens. Also, he states at the end of the essay that he wants to live without trouble. His upbringing has caused him to be negative, but at this point in his life, because he is old, he tends to be more cautious so as not to irritate anyone. Answers will vary as to readers' impressions of the author.

3. The fact that the author has always been a member of an ethnic minority has colored the way he thinks and has caused him to observe the world around him differently. This is a good linking device, for it keeps him constantly centered on his purpose in writing the essay.

4. The author supports his arguments well. He gives examples for each of his statements, i.e., how Americans behave on a bus or lobby for profit. Students will have various answers as to why his method of writing evokes an emotional response. It should be noted that his methods are inflammatory and easily evoke emotional responses (e.g., "The bad thing about America is that there is too much freedom," "Americans are so *careless* about so many things," or ". . . when people grow up, they only think of money and profits at the expense of everything else").

IV. Poetry: A Different Approach to Word Study

The following poems by Rose Anna Higashi ("Kinship"), Louise Erdrich ("Indian Boarding School: The Runaways"), Edwin Arlington Robinson ("Richard Cory"), and Janis Mirikitani ("Ms.") provide yet another way an instructor might approach rhetorical strategies and word usage in a composition classroom. Informative process analysis, for instance, could be taught by examining Louise Erdrich's poem "Indian Boarding School: The Runaways." Her objective is not to outline a method for running away from a boarding school (a "how to" use of process analysis); instead, she seeks to inform us of the process the speaker of the poem uses to escape the "Indian Boarding School." To teach illustration and example, one might note how Edwin Arlington Robinson uses the observations of the "townspeople" in "Richard Cory" to illustrate their superficial understanding of Cory as a human being.

All poetry selections include the same instructional apparatus provided with our expository writings within the text: Pre-reading and post-reading questions, along with collaborative and individualized exercises and writing activities. Thus, while your students might enjoy the change of pace of reading a poem, you have an opportunity to intensely examine imagery, symbolism and figurative language by studying some poetry in class.

ROSE ANNA HIGASHI

KINSHIP

Rose Anna Higashi is a professor of English, specializing in Japanese literature, English literature, and composition. Her poems appear in numerous magazines and journals, and her recent personal journal and poetry collection entitled *Blue Wines* was published by Paulist Press in 1995. Most recently, Higashi completed *Finding the Poet* (1996), a text on writing poetry and self-discovery. She has also written a novel, *Waiting for Rain*. Many people, places, and things have played a part in shaping Higashi's prose and poetry over the years: her hometown, Joplin, Missouri; authors Matsuo Basho, Gerard Manley Hopkins, and Robert Browning, and mysticism and spirituality.

Pre-reading Questions

1. What does the word kinship mean? If you are not sure, look up its various definitions in your dictionary.
2. How do people sometimes act or communicate if they feel awkward or are going through an awkward stage?

David tied on his tennis shoes,
Went out to the garage to get his skate board,
And after being reminded (by me), turned off the TV.
Then he rolled out the front door, quacking
"See ya later," in Donald Duck, a dialect
He has lately mastered
His best-quacked phrase being,
"You asked for it; you got it: Toyota."
And startlingly David finds no difficulty edging this
     expression
Into every conversation with me and other people
Who are important to him.
Donald Duck has saved our relationship.
Strange things can happen, as you must know, when a boy
     and his mother
Wear the same size hiking boots, and see each other
Almost eye to eye
The old contacts, napping together ten years ago,
(His soft fingers pinching the straps of my silky slip)
Can't go on and even words must change,

115

You know the wild abandon of young mothers
Speaking to sleeping babies
When their husbands are not in the room.
Quacking has helped.
Even last night,
As I handed David his sleeping bag over the back fence
So he could spend the night with the neighbors,
He quacked quietly to me in darkness,
"I love you."

Post-reading Questions

CONTENT

1. What symbolic meaning could the fence and the sleeping bag have in this poem?

2. The boy is beginning to develop his own independence separate from his mother. What does the mother do to assist him?

3. In your observation and experiences, do parents sometimes interfere with their children's attempts to live more independent lives? Has this ever happened to you or with others you know? In what way?

4. Higashi indicated in an interview that the theme of her poem is "family love." How does the son express his love for his mother? How does the mother express her love for her son?

STRATEGIES AND STRUCTURES

1. What strategy does Higashi use to emphasize parts of her poem that are the most important?

2. Who is the speaker in this poem and what effect does the conversational voice have on the reader? How and why might you call the conversational tone a "strategy" used to reinforce the theme of the poem?

3. How old is the boy in the poem? What words, lines, and phrases provide you with details, suggesting his age?

4. In what way might the boy's imitation of Donald Duck's voice be a symbolic or an indirect way of communicating with his "loved ones" (in this case, his mother)?

LANGUAGE AND VOCABULARY

1. Vocabulary: *dialect, abandoned*. What does the word dialect mean? In what way is her use of "dialect" ironic in this poem? What are the connotations of abandoned? Jot down your responses in your writing log.

2. Like many poets, Higashi uses figurative language in her poetry—that is, she employs language and phrases which
   communicate on a figurative rather than a literal level. Bearing this in mind, when the speaker says, "Donald Duck has
   saved our relationship," what does she really mean?

Group Activities

1. After you assemble in small groups, write a one-page description of a situation you experienced when you began to
   assert your own independence or helped someone else do
   so. Then, compare your experiences; what sort of things did
   your group share in common? How were they different?
   Can you draw any conclusions on the topic of gaining independence based on the material produced by the group?
   Explain.
2. Get into groups and brainstorm some of the ways that people (use yourselves as examples) borrow the identity of another person or character (such as Donald Duck) when
   they find it difficult to communicate directly. Have a group
   recorder write down your responses, and share them with
   your peers in a class forum.

Writing Assignments

1. Compose a brief narrative about an incident in your life in
   which your relationship with one of your parents clashed.
2. Write an expository essay comparing and contrasting the
   way you used to communicate with your parents to the
   way you communicate with them now.

Answer Key: Kinship

CONTENT

1. The purpose and effect of erecting a fence is privacy; a
   fence is a barrier. Symbolically, then, we might conclude
   that something now separates mother and son.
2. First and foremost, the mother in the poem gives her son
   permission to sleep at his friend's house, encouraging his
   independence. She also assists her son's development *rites
   of passage* (from dependence on family to self-reliance) by
   passing the sleeping bag over the fence so he can sleep at a
   neighbor's house.
3. Answers to this question will vary.
4. The son actually tells his mother he loves her at the end of
   the poem. The duck dialect which he uses also seems to be

an endearment expressing a special affection for her. In contrast, the mother demonstrates her love by "letting go," allowing her son to begin to carve his own individuality and independence. Passing the sleeping bag over the fence could symbolize this. He is beginning to take care of himself.

STRATEGIES AND STRUCTURES

1.   Among other strategies, Higashi uses short lines to emphasize and draw attention to the most important sections in her poem.

2.   The mother is the speaker in this poem—reflecting on her past relationship with her son. The conversational, matter-of-fact tone of the poem nicely complements the general theme of communication. (It might be interesting to point out the several different types of communication going on in the poem.)

3.   The boy in the poem is most likely around 13 years old. The poet reveals this information right after stating that "Donald Duck has saved our relationship." She notes that she and her son are about the same size—"wear the same size hiking boots," and "see each other / Almost eye to eye."

4.   Speaking in strange voices to a loved one can be a way of showing one's affection. Consider how first-time mothers and fathers make all sorts of silly noises or else use "baby-talk" when attempting to communicate with their children. In a like manner, when the boy adopts a duck dialect, quacking to his mother and others close to him, he subconsciously (perhaps consciously) is selecting a special personae for communicating with those he cares about.

LOUISE ERDRICH

INDIAN BOARDING SCHOOL: THE RUNAWAYS

Of Chippewa and German-American descent, Louise Erdrich frequently writes about the Native American experience. Both a poet and a novelist, she has had many of her works published in such magazines as *Esquire, Chicago, Paris Review, Antaeus, Georgia Review, Redbook, Ms.*, and *Frontiers*. Erdrich's published works include *Jacklight* (1984), *Baptism of Desire* (1989), collections of poetry, and several novels: *Love Medicine* (1984), *The Beet Queen* (1986), and *Tracks* (1988). In 1992, Erdrich published *The Crown of Columbus,* a novel she co-authored with her recently deceased husband, Michael Dorris. Among her most recent works are *The Blue Jay's Dance: A Birth Year* (1995), a nonfiction work regarding small and large events all parents will relate to, and *Tales of Burning Love* (1996), which has been described as "not so much as a novel, but a study of passion" since it "explores the possibilities of love through a collection of reminiscences of four women who have been married to the same man." The following poem is a selection from *Jacklight*.

Pre-reading Questions

1. Cluster or brainstorm the words "boarding school" and "runaway." What are the emotional qualities you associate with each word group?
2. In your opinion, what are the characteristics of shame? What are some of the ways people and institutions in our society make others feel shame?

Home is the place we head for in our sleep.
Boxcars stumbling north in dreams
don't wait for us. We catch them on the run.
The rails, old lacerations that we love,
shoot parallel across the face and break
just under Turtle Mountains. Riding scars
you can't get lost. Home is the place they cross.

The lame guard strikes a match and makes the dark
less tolerant. We watch through cracks in boards
as the land starts rolling, rolling till it hurts
to be here, cold in regulation clothes.
We know the sheriff's waiting at midrun
to take us back. His car is numb and warm.

The highway doesn't rock, it only hums
like a wing of long insults. The worn-down welts
of ancient punishments lead back and forth.

All runaways wear dresses, long green ones,
the color you would think shame was. We scrub
the sidewalks down because it's shameful work.
Our brushes cut the stone in watered arcs
and in the soak frail outlines shiver clear
a moment, things us kids pressed on the dark
face before it hardened, pale, remembering
delicate old injuries, the spines of names and leaves.

Post-reading Questions

CONTENT

1. Where do the Indian runaways "head for"?
2. What does Erdrich mean by "Riding scars / you can't get lost"?
3. The word "regulation" implies conformity and order. What did you immediately picture when you read the words "regulation clothes"? Why?
4. Erdrich says: "All runaways wear dresses, long green ones / the color you would think shame was." If *shame* had to be a color, why might it be green?

STRATEGIES AND STRUCTURES

1. How does Erdrich's stanza division depict three different stages of running away?
2. What is the strategic purpose for comparing a ride on a boxcar to a ride in the sheriff's car?
3. Why does Erdrich constantly refer to pain or use the results of a painful incident (e.g., scar) as figurative images throughout her poem?
4. The poet often refers to insults, shame, and ancient injuries and punishments. What do they tell you about Native Americans and how they feel about themselves?

LANGUAGE AND VOCABULARY

1. Underline instances where Erdrich employs personification (using human qualities to describe non-humans) in her poem. Then write five original sentences using personification in your journal or writing log (try to write a poem!)
2. In a short paragraph, analyze what *you think* Erdrich was referring to figuratively and literally in the last line of the third stanza: ". . . remembering / delicate old injuries, the spines of names and leaves."

Group Activities

1. Go through the poem line by line and determine the *meaning* Erdrich was attempting to convey; then, paraphrase each stanza of her verse.
2. Using three stanzas as Louise Erdrich does, write a collaborative poem describing when and where you planned and did something (e.g., staying home from work to go to a concert or sneaking out of your parents' house), got caught, and how you were punished.

Writing Activities

1. Write about a time in your life when you planned or actually did run away from home. How did you go about planning your "escape"? What eventually happened?
2. Compose a humorous essay wherein you explain the best process for running away from home, getting out of a relationship, breaking out of a hospital, or escaping a maximum-security prison. Since your composition will be a directional process essay, it will be important to include transitional devices to lead your reader from one step to the next.

Answer Key: Indian Boarding School: The Runaways

CONTENT
1. According to Erdrich, Indian runaways head for home ("Home is the place we head for in our sleep").
2. The allusion to scars in this poem literally refers to the railroad tracks but symbolically could be a representation of one's memory of bad experiences (scars) or the pain that runaways feel when they know that they have no real chance of ever making it to the place they call home.
3. Answers will vary.
4. Answers will vary, but one possible explanation could be shame grows, with growth being represented by the color green.

STRATEGIES AND STRUCTURES
1. In each stanza of this three-stanza poem, Erdrich presents different themes: (1) escape, (2) pursuit, and (3) capture. The initial stanza suggests excitement and positive expectations. In stanza two, however, the bubble bursts because they know what to expect halfway through their journey but are willing to take a chance anyway. Stanza three dashes all of their hopes in that they are captured, returned, and forced to perform shameful activities to atone for their disregard for authority.

2. Although one must endure hardships to achieve the illusive quality of freedom, one is quite willing to do so as demonstrated by the most uncomfortable journey on the train. Ironically, however, a comfortable ride back to the boarding school in the sheriff's car is far more painful than their train ride because it will produce mental and spiritual anguish from which there is no hope of escape.

3. Regardless of where the runaways are in this poem, they always are suffering from some sort of pain. The allusion to scars may indicate the severity of the injuries, especially those that are mental.

4. The American Indians have been taught that their customs, religion, and mores are unacceptable in a "civilized" society. As a result, they have low self-esteem, no sense of dignity, and no hope of a future living off-reservation.

EDWIN ARLINGTON ROBINSON

RICHARD CORY

Robinson grew up in Gardiner, Maine, which was the scene of several of his poems. He could afford only two years of college and struggled to support himself until President Theodore Roosevelt took an interest in his work and got him a job as a clerk. A winner of three Pulitzer Prizes for poetry, Robinson's works include *Children of the Night* (1897) and *Collected Poems* (1922).

Pre-reading Questions

1. How does money solve some problems while creating others?
2. Have you ever envied a person for being wealthy, beautiful, or handsome?
3. Do you tend to think of these people in a stereotypical way (e.g., the wealthy have no problems, or beautiful people are always popular and happy)? Why?

Whenever Richard Cory went down town,
We people on the pavement looked at him;
He was a gentleman from sole to crown,
Clean favored, and imperially slim.

And he was always quietly arrayed,
And he was always human when he talked;
But still he fluttered pulses when he said,
"Good-morning," and he glittered when he walked.

And he was rich—yes, richer than a king—
And admirably schooled in every grace:
In fine, we thought that he was everything
To make us wish that we were in his place.

So on we worked, and waited for the light,
And went without the meat, and cursed the bread;
And Richard Cory, one calm summer night,
Went home and put a bullet through his head.

Post-reading Questions

CONTENT

1. Why do the townspeople want to be like Richard Cory? What do they see in him that they feel they lack?

2. How does the narrator of the poem view Richard Cory? Do the townspeople make any attempts to understand or relate to Richard Cory as a person? Why or why not?

3. Considering the information given to you in the first 14 lines of the poem, how do you think the people reacted to Cory's suicide?

4. The narrator makes his conclusion about Cory based on *what* Cory looks like and *how* Cory speaks. By basing his opinions on physical appearance and what Cory says in casual conversation, the narrator (townspeople) has neatly categorized Cory, which does not allow him to be a "normal" person. As a result of this, what is your opinion of the townspeople?

STRATEGIES AND STRUCTURES

1. What is the effect of starting successive lines with the word *and* (lines 5, 6, 10, 11, 14, and 15)? What have you always been told about beginning a sentence with the word *and*?

2. How does the poet suggest from the beginning of the poem that something has happened to Richard Cory?

3. What illustrations and examples does the poet use in his description of Cory? Which of his senses does the poet use in the description (hearing, sight, taste, smell, and touch)?

4. As mentioned in the Narration Chapter, poems often are like mini-essays. How does each stanza in Robinson's poem function like a paragraph? What is the purpose of the first line in each stanza (groupings of lines in a poem, e.g., two lines grouped together are a couplet and four lines are a quatrain)?

LANGUAGE AND VOCABULARY

1. Vocabulary: *imperially slim, quietly arrayed, sole to crown, admirably schooled.* The above words should not be viewed separately but as a unit, and each unit functions as an adjective which describes Richard Cory. Using the word units above and five more of your own, write a one- to two-paragraph description of a member of your class.

2. When writing poems, poets often use *figures of speech* (departures from the normal meaning of language). In "Richard Cory," Robinson gives us one of the best examples of a figure of speech, *irony,* which is an expression with a contrast

between the apparent and intended meaning of the words. What does Robinson want us to assume about Cory? Why are we shocked when Cory commits suicide? How is this a good example of irony? Write your own example of irony in your notebook.

Group Activities

1. Pair off with another member of the class and glance over your notes from Vocabulary, "Activity a." Spend some time observing people on campus, and choose one particular person to concentrate on. Write a collaborative description of this person using adjective units similar to those you developed in the vocabulary exercise, and then, in a second paragraph, you and your partner will make assumptions about that person based entirely on your observations. Do not engage this person in conversation or try to get to know him or her.

2. Cluster and/or brainstorm the issue of *misunderstanding* as a class, recording the results of your work on the blackboard. Next, get into smaller groups and decide which of the issues listed on the board are the easiest to write about. Select what your group considers the three most important topics and construct a thesis statement for each, and outline how you would use illustration and example to support your thesis.

Writing Activities

1. Compose an original thesis that says something *about* the theme of *appearance versus reality.* Support what you say with examples drawn from personal observation, experience, and readings. Try to use all three types of illustration mentioned at the beginning of this chapter.

2. Write an essay in which you reveal something about yourself by writing about another person. First, deal with how you react to the person's physical appearance. Next, include how other people see and feel about this person. Prior to your final draft, revise any portion of your paper where you could use an active verb or a concrete noun.

3. Compare and contrast Robinson's portrait of Richard Cory to similar social figures in contemporary society; the person/persons need not have committed suicide. . . . However, you may want to consider actions by each individual that are different than yet similar to Cory in order to draw

some "probable" conclusions about the human condition. (People like Donald Trump—as well as multi-millionaire celebrities would be ideal examples.)

Answer Key: Richard Cory

CONTENT

1. The townspeople want to be like Cory because he is rich, handsome, and a gentleman. Basically, he is what they aspire to be.
2. The narrator, like the townspeople, puts Richard Cory on a pedestal and never sees him as an actual human being. A person with all of Cory's qualities never seems to be quite natural.
3. Obviously the townspeople were devastated by Cory's suicide because they were in such awe of him.
4. Answers may vary but should be based on the fact that the townspeople have made superficial judgments about Cory.

STRATEGIES AND STRUCTURES

1. By starting lines 5, 6, 10, 11, 14, and 15 with the conjunction "and," Robinson creates a sense of urgency, i.e., he piles quality upon quality, building our expectations and our mental image of Cory as a person.
2. The poet uses the past tense to suggest that something has happened to Richard Cory.
3. Robinson appeals to such senses as sight (imperially slim), sound (he was always human when he talked), touch (fluttered pulses), and taste (went without the meat, and cursed the bread).
4. Each stanza in Robinson's poem functions the same as a paragraph because each gives a description of some aspect of Cory's behavior, and the first lines function as topic sentences.

JANICE MIRIKITANI

Ms.

Janice Mirikitani is a third-generation Japanese-American poet. She is renowned for her explosive poetry dealing with racial and sexual stereotypes. In addition to such works as *Shedding Silence, Poetry and Prose* (1987), Mirikitani has edited several anthologies, including *Ayumi: The Japanese-American Anthology* and *Third World Woman*.

Pre-reading Questions

1. If you are female, what does the title "Ms." mean to you? Do you insist on being called Ms.? If you are a male, how do you react to calling a woman "Ms."?
2. Do titles like Mr., Mrs., Miss, Master, or Ms. influence the way you think about somebody? Does a title influence the way you feel about yourself? Explain.

I got into a thing
with someone
because I called her
miss ann/kennedy/rockerfeller/hughes
instead of ms.
I said
it was a waste of time
worrying about it.

her cool blue eyes
iced me—a victim of sexism.

I wanted to accommodate her
and call her what she deserved.
but knowing that would please her
instead
i said,

> *white lace & satin was never soiled by*
> *sexism*
> *sheltered as you are by mansions*
> *built on Indian land*

> *your diamonds shipped with slaves from Africa*
> *your underwear washed by Chinese laundries*
> *your house cleaned by my grandmother*

so do not push me any further.

and when you quit
killing us for democracy
and stop calling ME gook

I will call you
whatever you like.

Post-reading Questions

CONTENT

1. There seems to be a conflict in this poem. What exactly is it? Who is involved in this struggle?
2. What role does accommodation play in this poem? Why does the poet decide *not* to call ann/kennedy/rockerfeller/ hughes "Ms."?
3. What is the ultimate irony in this poem? What does "Ms." stand for? Is there a male equivalent for this word? Is there a male equivalent for Miss?

STRATEGIES AND STRUCTURES

1. The poem begins with a reference to sexism; where does it lead us? What are the relationships between the two?
2. What is the effect of the extended use of the first-person "I" in the first few stanzas of the poem? Whom does the reader focus upon?
3. What changes in meaning result when the poet shifts to second-person "you" and "your"?

LANGUAGE AND VOCABULARY

1. Vocabulary: *accommodate, sexism, democracy.* Although most of these words already are familiar to you, the three words above are central to the meaning of the poem. Can you think of any way to accommodate sexism and racism in a democratic society? (Obviously, you will have to look into the meanings of these words more fully than just a quick glance at a pocket dictionary.) Compose one or two paragraphs showing how sexism and racism can or cannot be accommodated by members of a democracy.
2. What is the effect of specific concrete images (e.g., "diamonds shipped with slaves from Africa") in the poem?

Group Activities

1. As a class, discuss what Kennedy, Rockefeller, and Hughes (Howard) have in common. What does the poet's reference

to these individuals in place of Ann's last name suggest about her? Why do you imagine she uses lower-case letters regardless of whose name she mentions?

2. Each member of the class will spend a week addressing every female he/she encounters as Ms. At the end of the week, meet in small groups and discuss how each female reacted to being addressed in this manner. (Be sure to keep a record of each reaction.) Overall, were the reactions to being called Ms. favorable, indifferent, or hostile? What sorts of people reacted favorably, indifferently, or hostilely? What can your group conclude about forms of address?

Writing Activities

1. Write a cause–effect essay discussing the title of Mirikitani's poem, "Ms." Does the use of this word in society eliminate the causes of sexism, or does the use of it gloss over the deeper problems experienced by women, single or married, in our society?

2. Like Mirikitani, we often state that something is "a waste of time," and yet we spend a great deal of effort arguing and worrying about it. Write about an encounter with someone which caused you to become upset and do or say things that you felt were a waste of time. Analyze the reason for your discomfort, and state whether your efforts justified the stress that you encountered.

Answer Key: Ms.

CONTENT

1. The conflict deals with racism between suppressed women of diverse cultures in America: one belongs to an ethnic group; the other is a member of western culture but, nonetheless, is still oppressed.

2. The Caucasian woman is not accommodating to Mirikitani, an Asian. That is, she does not acknowledge her own role in perpetuating racism. Nevertheless, the Caucasian woman expects Mirikitani to accommodate her by addressing her as Ms. Essentially, Mirikitani is saying, "I'll acknowledge your hardships resulting from sexism (which Mirikitani, being female, no doubt shares) when you acknowledge my struggle with racism."

3. The ultimate irony of the poem resides in the fact that a woman who professes to be liberated and acknowledges her culture's own suppression has not, according to the poet, recognized the fact that women of western culture, while oppressed themselves, promote or promoted racism.

The title "Ms." stands for "myself," and is a title free of reference to marital status which women use. The male equivalent of Ms. would be Mr.

STRATEGIES AND STRUCTURES

1. The poem begins with a reference to sexism and leads to a discussion of racism. Both are unfair, lead to stereotypes, and deny a person dignity and identity. The dominant culture in American society has been both racist and sexist. Historically, feminists and civil rights advocates have often worked together to fight oppression in its many forms (something the poet does not acknowledge).

2. Through the repetition of the word "I," the reader remains clearly focused on the poet's reactions to the request of a Westerner to use the title Ms.

3. After speaking in first person, taking on the burdens of her race, Mirikitani moves from her own feeling to another's actions.

V. Practices, Purposes, and Exercises in Writing

Integrating Technology into the Writing Process

JOCELYN S. YOUNG
Evergreen Valley College

Variations on Writing Assignments

MARK NICHOLL-JOHNSON
Merced College

JOCELYN S. YOUNG

INTEGRATING TECHNOLOGY
INTO THE WRITING PROCESS

I recently came across a recruiting advertisement for a major data technology company in the newspaper. It read: "What Good Is It . . . If It's Not Innovative?" Indeed, exciting reports of technological innovations permeate the hi-tech world. And integrating technology into education has become a top priority for many educational institutions, especially as schools embrace the challenge of preparing students for the twenty-first century. In fact, research shows that to be competitive in the workplace, graduating students must possess not only basic skills—such as reading, writing, and mathematics skills—but also new types of skills, such as computer literacy, interpersonal skills, and what is often termed "big picture vision." To effectively equip students with these skills, colleges and universities themselves must incorporate educational technology into their classrooms. Yet successful use of technology in the classroom need not be more than a modest effort to integrate one form of technology into existing lesson plans. In fact, the most successful uses of technology in the classroom occur when instructors view technology as a *tool* to enhance teaching, a tool that adds another dimension to existing teaching methods and materials in the curriculum. One technological application that offers a wealth of resources for English instructors is the Internet, to which more and more schools are gaining access.

By incorporating the Internet into curriculum that encourages an active approach to research, reading, and writing, composition instructors illustrate to their students that the writing process itself consists of much more than simply writing: the development of reading, discussion, and critical thinking skills supports and complements the writing process. Fundamental to the development of reading (and writing) skills are primary source materials, such as newspapers, government documents, photographs, and even original prose and poetry. Fortunately, the Internet makes available much information previously accessible to only a limited audience. For instance, institutions worldwide have placed their publications on-line. Many major newspapers, such as the *New York Times* (http://www.nytimes.com/) and the *Christian Science Monitor* (http://www.csmonitor.com/) are available in on-line editions. In fact, a simple Internet search reveals that there are over 1000 newspapers on the Internet. Some remain free of charge to users; others require a subscription. And the federal government is in the process of converting many of its publications into an electronic format; the research libraries of major universities provide links to electronic government document resources. Even many museums of art and photography maintain web sites, some including exhibitions and others listing art-related resources. Requiring students to include at least one or two resources from the Internet in their research assignments introduces students to the wealth of available resources.

Using the Internet in teaching can supplement many discussion-based and collaborative activity lesson plans. Such activities seek to actively engage more students, possessing a diversity of talents, interests, and academic backgrounds, in the learning process. Using the interface of the Internet can be especially effective in encouraging more students to participate. Many instructors use the Internet to foster dialogue among students outside of class. Some instructors require their students to have a campus e-mail account (where available) to facilitate class announcements and feedback. Other instructors set up an on-line discussion forum for their students to enter thoughts and reflections on class time and class readings. Still other instructors post the course materials on their school web site. That way, even though most instructors still provide their students with hard copies of the course materials, students can always access another copy of a reading through the web site. On their own, students can subscribe to on-line resources such as e-mail discussion lists for writing and composition.

Even schools with limited technological resources can take advantage of classroom conferencing or collaborative writing software to increase interactivity among students. Such software applications, for example *Aspects* or *ClassWriter,* do not require a file server or even on-line access. How practical instructors find such software applications varies greatly. For example, *Aspects* allows instructors to create a conference, or a number of conferences, among computers connected with a network—even among computers connected to a shared printer—not necessarily with a file server. Instructors can choose the desired level of mediation among conference participants, ranging from "free for all" mediation, in which every student can edit at the same time (in separate paragraphs), to "full mediation," in which only one person at a time can edit. The software application *ClassWriter* encourages collaborative inquiry and writing among students of English. *ClassWriter* consists of two programs, Electronic Dialectical Notebook and Conversation, each of which contributes to the process of collaborative inquiry. In the Electronic Dialectical Notebook program, instructors provide source material ("scripts") to focus students' inquiries and responses, while instructors play more of a facilitator role in the Conversation program, directing, redirecting, and contributing to the dialogue among students. However composition instructors choose to integrate these or similar software applications in their classrooms, challenging students to write in different settings and for different audiences is a valuable teaching strategy that can be enhanced through technological applications.

Teaching students how to navigate their way through the web of information on the Internet at once poses great challenges and benefits for instructors and students. On one hand, the sheer amount of information on the Internet affords students access to information previously inaccessible to a general audience. At the same time, though, students are faced with the enormous challenge of sifting through the hoards of results one gets from a search: for example, searching for the term "smoking" in one search engine turns up over 20,000 resources. Of course, these search results range from personal web pages describing one's efforts to quit smoking to a sports article entitled, "Hot and Smoking." Continually refining search terms requires critical thinking as students must select their sources carefully, asking questions like: What web site did this link come from? Who wrote this article? What other sources can support this information? Relatively uncensored, the Internet demands that students make critical choices, distinguishing between fact and fiction and evaluating the reliability of the information they find. If sifting through the "garbage" information on the Internet simply is not practical for your class, introduce your students to the growing number of sites created by libraries. Because libraries are critical of the materials they select to include in their catalogs, web sites created by libraries will likely contain more veritable sources of information.

MARK NICHOLL-JOHNSON
VARIATIONS ON WRITING ASSIGNMENTS

Although students in any basic writing course may be placed together because as writers they work on more or less the same level, similar writing proficiency doesn't, obviously, mean that students have anything else in common—especially a coherent body of academic or cultural information. This heterogeneity of experience virtually guarantees that there will be no common language (in every sense of the word) in the classroom, despite what might be inferred from the identification of the course as one in "English." The three assignment guidelines that follow begin with the assumptions that (1) students in a basic writing class have little if anything in common, (2) that the energy expended by any attempt to furnish them with a common body of academic or cultural information in a basic writing class would be better spent in the effort to get students to think about whatever they already do know, and (3) to write this knowledge in ways that approach the methods of academic discourse. In an ideal world, such assignments, of course, would not be necessary.

The following assignments were devised in an attempt to find a common denominator for class assignments that would move in the direction of academic discourse, be challenging and interesting for everyone, and yet would not exclude the non-native speaker of English—whose experiences, academic or other, may as yet be untranslated into English (and who, additionally, may have little or no formal education in any language). The first of these assignments relies on mapping as a non-verbal way of jogging memory to generate information for a short paper. The second two assignments begin by focusing on childhood experiences that seem to be almost universal (listening to stories and playing games) and then proceed by analyzing these experiences through a series of simple questions.

ASSIGNMENT 1: MAPPING A PLACE (DESCRIPTION)

After reading a selection that features the description of a place, I often ask students to make a map of the place described, which requires them to pay close attention to the language used by the writer to establish spatial relationships. This mapping exercise works to show student readers that writers use techniques of spatial organization to organize descriptive passages. This activity presents other benefits to student writers. Very often, for example, second-language students find it difficult to make distinctions among prepositions such as in/on/at, and this exercise may help them to see how words such as these work when used precisely. If students work in groups, non-native speakers can often learn quite a bit from native speakers of English, and these native speakers may enjoy the challenge of having to explain things about the language that they have probably taken for granted.

Once students have made maps revealing information they have gleaned from reading, I ask them to take part of a class hour to map a place that they know well—their current or former neighborhood, for instance. This activity produces an interesting variety of visualizations, with students occasionally working in painstaking detail while others are content with very simple sketch-maps. When they have completed these maps, I ask them to talk for a few minutes about them with a partner or in a group, and encourage the listeners to ask questions. Once everyone has had a chance to talk about his or her map, I begin a series of brief writings about the place. This might include a freewriting about the place in general, one that focuses on what seems most important or interesting about it, and so forth. Eventually, students will produce a short paper in which they describe a place that is important or interesting. My experience has been that sequenced exercises asking students to read-map-talk-write usually helps students to produce writing that makes a point, and is reasonably well-developed and organized.

ASSIGNMENT 2: ANALYZING AN ORAL STORY (NARRATION)

An exercise I have used to move beyond the personal narrative involves asking students to retell a story they have been told as a child and eventually, engage in a sort of analysis of it. Preliminary work involves talking about the variety of uses to which stories are put—to entertain, to teach, to remember, and so forth—and the variety of forms they may take. For this assignment, it is important for me to stress that the story must be one that was told to the students, not one they had read, seen on TV or in the movies, or even one that was read to them.

The first step is to recall stories that one might tell, and then to choose one and retell it. This retelling might first be oral, told in class to a partner or a group. Then I ask students to write the story. Once a draft of the story is on paper, I present some questions to the class as follows:

- What were the circumstances of the story? That is, who told it to you, when, where and for what purpose?
- What was your response, or what did this story mean to you when you first heard it? Do you understand the story differently now?
- Would you retell this story to a child now? Why or why not? What, if anything, would you change about it? Why would(n't) you change it?

Having written a draft of the story and responses to these questions, students are ready to compose a paper in which they retell and discuss a story they had been told as children. This leads to the exploration of various problems of organization, emphasis, interpretation, etc. that students must confront in completing such an assignment. I have found this assignment particularly rewarding to many Southeast Asian students who, although often lacking extensive formal education, have grown up in a lively oral tradition.

ASSIGNMENT 3: ANALYZING A GAME (PROCESS OR PROCEDURE)

An assignment similar to this one involves the explanation of a game students remember from childhood. The basic ground rule for this assignment is that the game must be one learned from other children, not from adults, or at least that it was learned by playing rather than by reading about it. That means, for example, that students will not be explaining the rules of baseball, but rather of varieties of baseball played in neighborhoods: three flies up, over the line, pickle, hit the bat, etc. If students can't think of anything but board games like Monopoly, I ask them to consider family or local variations on the official rules, e.g., the officially unauthorized but widely practiced gambit of putting money collected from taxes and fines on the board to be recovered by a lucky player who lands on Free Parking.

The procedure for working through this assignment is similar to that for the childhood story above. This time, of course, the goal is to produce a set of instructions that would inform a reader on how to play the game. Questions I ask students to answer are:

* When and where did you play this game?
* How did you learn to play?
* What equipment was necessary?
* How were disputes settled?
* Have you seen children playing this game as you did?

As with the story assignment, students then work on composing a paper about a childhood game in which they explain the games and discuss it in terms (some or all) of the questions above. For this assignment, they are confronted with problems of explaining procedures, rather than narrative as they present information.

VI. Selected Quizzes

Quiz—Saigon, April, 1975

1. When the author rushed to the roof of his house, saw the reddish glows and heard the rumbling of artillery, what did he know would inevitably happen?

2. What had happened to his wife's relatives during the Hue horror of Tet, 1968?

3. Why did his wife change her mind about escaping? What did they do to try to escape?

4. Why was their first attempt at escape unsuccessful? Where did they go then?

5. Why did the author think, "American aid was finally reaching the people"?

6. Why did the author feel that the world he had known for 28 years had ended abruptly?

7. Why is it ironic that General Minh called the Viet Cong "our brothers of the provisional government"?

8. Why was the author's father glad that they had not escaped?

9. Why did the author begin burning his uniforms and any pictures of him in uniform?

10. **DEFINE** each of the following words and **USE EACH IN A SENTENCE:**

    a. imminent

    b. ominous

    c. palpable

    d. incriminating

    e. provisional

Quiz—Champion of the World

1. Why did people keep wedging themselves into Uncle Willie's store?

2. Why did the author wonder if the radio announcer knew what he was doing when calling everybody "Ladies and gentlemen"?

3. Who was the "Brown Bomber"?

4. What would the old Christian ladies do if the "Brown Bomber" won the fight?

5. Why did the author and her brother Bailey place the coins on top of the cash register?

6. When it seemed as if the "Brown Bomber" were going down, why did everyone groan?

7. Why was everyone so excited when the "Brown Bomber" won?

8. How did people celebrate when the fight was over?

9. Why did those who lived too far away make arrangements to stay in town that night?

10. **DEFINE** each of the following words and **USE EACH IN A SENTENCE:**

    a. wedge (verb)

    b. cackled (like a hen)

    c. assent

    d. ambush

    e. contender

Quiz—Notes from a Son to His Father

1. How does the author feel about being a son?

2. Regardless of how Leong feels about his father, what does he usually find himself doing?

3. How does Leong "know" his father (how does he visualize him)?

4. What were his father's hands always busy doing?

5. Even though his father's hands are always busy, why does Leong not know the true strength of his father's arm?

6. Why is his father standing at the door to Leong's room? What does he hold in his hand?

7. How does Leong react? (What does he do?)

8. What does his father do, and why does Leong despise his father even more?

9. Why does Leong feel that his father is not as good as Abraham?

10. **DEFINE** each of the following words and **USE EACH IN A SENTENCE:**

    a. inanimate

    b. vengeance

    c. dispassion

    d. seething

    e. fibrous

Quiz—Old Before Her Time

1. How old was Patty Moore and how old did she become when she transformed herself?

2. What motivated Patty to make her strange journey?

3. What happened when Patty attended a gerontology conference disguised as an old woman? What lesson did Patty learn at this conference?

4. When she was attacked in New York City, what lesson did she learn?

5. What lesson did she learn on the slushy, gray day in New York?

6. What lesson did she learn from the lady whose husband hit her?

7. What lesson did she learn when she dressed as an old bag lady?

8. What lesson did she learn from the woman who said, "It's been a long time since anyone hugged me"?

9. What lesson did she learn from the gentleman on the park bench?

10. **DEFINE** each of the following words and **USE EACH IN A SENTENCE:**

    a. abysmal

    b. deteriorate

    c. condescending

    d. disillusion

    e. audible

Quiz—Confessions of a Quit Addict

1. Who was Timothy Leary and what did he want his followers to do?

2. Why did the author have little trouble following Leary's chant?

3. Who became her collaborator?

4. How did the author and her collaborator escape from the American society at that time?

5. Where were they living when she decided she needed to change her life again?

6. Graham decided that the problem wasn't in the places they went or people they found, but in what?

7. What did the author do then?

8. In the past, Graham went looking for change. What does she now realize about change?

9. Why doesn't the author like to consider herself a "recovering" quitter?

10. **DEFINE** each of the following words and **USE EACH IN A SENTENCE:**

    a. collaborator

    b. redemption

    c. tenacious

    d. superficial

    e. nirvana

QUIZ—MYTH OF THE MODEL MINORITY

1. According to the author, what have Chinese Americans been known as?

2. What happened in Pasadena that shows a different side to the Chinese American?

3. What is the "silver screen" and what images of the Chinese American did it present in the past?

4. What did the Chinese become to the Americans during World War II?

5. When the Korean War took place, how did Americans view the Chinese?

6. Who visited China in 1972 and what was the U.S.'s view of China then?

7. What is the author "fed up" with in connection with Chinese Americans?

8. What is the author proud of?

9. How does the author want the media to view Chinese Americans?

10. **DEFINE** each of the following words and **USE EACH IN A SENTENCE:**

   a. insidious

   b. amiable

   c. inscrutable

   d. manifestation

   e. conscientiously

Quiz—The Ways We Lie

1. How many lies did the author tell in the course of one day without feeling the least bit guilty?

2. What happened when the author went an entire week without telling a lie?

3. What is a white lie?

4. What is a "façade," and how can it be dangerous?

5. What is "deflecting," and how do "deflectors" act when accused of "inappropriate behavior"?

6. What are stereotypes, and why are they so dangerous?

7. Why does the author like "out-and-out lies" the best?

8. Why can the roots of many mental disorders be traced back to the "dismissal of reality"?

9. What is delusion, and how is it a survival mechanism which we all use?

10. **DEFINE** each of the following words and **USE EACH IN A SENTENCE:**

    a. embellish

    b. perpetuate

    c. gamut

    d. renegade

    e. harassment

QUIZ—WHAT IS POVERTY

1. What are the smells of poverty? (Name three.)

2. What happened to her children the last time the author had a job?

3. What is the author's answer to people who say, "Anybody can be clean"?

4. What happened when the author saved for two months for a jar of Vaseline?

5. What is poverty in the winter? In the summer?

6. What happens when the author asks for help?

7. When she asked for help, how much money did she finally receive? What did she use it for?

8. What kind of future do her children have? Why?

9. What does she dream of? Why are her dreams so different from those of people with money?

10. **DEFINE** each of the following words and **USE EACH IN A SENTENCE:**

    a. enslaved

    b. chronic

    c. antihistamines

    d. immoral

    e. illegitimate

QUIZ—DOES AMERICA STILL EXIST?

1. What does Rodriguez mean when he states, "Children of immigrant parents are supposed to perch on a hyphen between two countries?

2. Even though America is joined in a common culture, what doe the author mean when he says that we stand together, alone?

3. What, according to Rodriguez, most truly represents America?

4. List at least two ways in which Mexico contrasts with the United States.

5. What is a *mestizo*?

6. Even though the author states that the melting pot is retired, why does he say the process of assimilation is inevitable?

7. How do the children of immigrant parents become what their parents "could never have been"?

8. Why does Rodriguez feel the 1960s were so important to American history? What has happened since that era?

9. With whom do teenagers associate in high school? What happens once they graduate and join the working world?

10. **DEFINE** each of the following words and **USE EACH IN A SENTENCE:**

    a. assimilation

    b. inarticulate

    c. reciprocal

    d. exuberance

    e. bureaucratic

1. What did the author decide to do for her "first illusion of freedom" in 1966?

2. What did some people think was her reason for going to a white school?

3. What was her real reason for attending the school?

4. Even though she was escorted to school by national guardsmen, what happened at the entrance?

5. What was displayed on the signs the protesters were carrying?

6. What went on when she went to her first classes?

7. When she went to her last class, geometry, how was she feeling? How did the teacher treat her?

8. Why does she blame herself for that crushing moment?

9. What does freedom now mean to Jarrett?

10. **DEFINE** each of the following words and **USE EACH IN A SENTENCE:**

    a. desegregation

    b. denigrating

    c. emancipation

    d. futile

    e. irate

QUIZ—A HOMEMADE EDUCATION

1. Why was Malcolm X imprisoned?

2. With whom did Malcolm X correspond and what did this relationship lead to?

3. Even though Malcolm X's father was a preacher, where did he spend most of his life and what did he do before being sent to prison?

4. What was the last grade he attended and why did he decide to further his education?

5. How did he increase his vocabulary?

6. Why was he immensely proud of himself the morning after he began his studies?

7. What is an aardvark?

8. Not only did his vocabulary increase but also something else became better. What was it?

9. Once his vocabulary increased, what did he begin to do? As a result, even though he was imprisoned, how did he feel (for the first time in his life)?

10. **DEFINE** each of the following words and **USE EACH IN A SENTENCE:**

    a. emulate

    b. inevitable

    c. articulate

    d. riffling

    e. hustler

QUIZ—PERSPECTIVES ON BORDERS

1. Valdez thinks it is curious that the Mayan word for America is what?

2. The author states that the Mayas were able to predict the future. What was one of their predictions?

3. What did the Mayas, who were brilliant mathematicians, invent?

4. What did the Iroquois have that led to the concept of the U.S. government?

5. What is the meaning of the term "*Homo sapiens*"?

6. What is the symbol of intelligence in the *Popol Vuh,* the Mayan bible?

7. Even though some people want to declare English as the official language of the U.S., what can't they keep from happening?

8. Before the Europeans came to America, the evolution of this continent always involved migration in what direction?

9. To Valdez, what represents the promise of America?

10. **DEFINE** each of the following words and **USE EACH IN A SENTENCE:**

    a.   serpent

    b.   hemisphere

    c.   seduction

    d.   intimidate

    e.   confederacy

Quiz—Neat People vs. Sloppy People

1. What does the author feel is the difference between neat and sloppy people?

2. What are sloppy people always planning on doing "someday"?

3. Why don't sloppy people ever become neat?

4. How would a neat person clean a desk? How would a sloppy person do it?

5. Neat people operate on TWO principles. What are they?

6. What is the only messy item in a neat person's house?

7. How do neat people go through their mail?

8. Why are neat people no good to borrow from?

9. What do neat people do with the following and WHY?

    a. geranium

    b. the dog

    c. the children

10. **DEFINE** each of the following words and **USE EACH IN A SENTENCE:**

    a. rectitude

    b. mementos

    c. excavation

    d. meticulously

    e. distinction

QUIZ—LABOR AND CAPITAL:
THE COMING CATASTROPHE

1. Who is Carlos Bulosan and what jobs has he had?

2. What does the author think is the issue of the day?

3. Where does the author feel all the wealth of industrial countries is concentrated?

4. In the U.S., who produces the wealth and who distributes it?

5. What do the contradictions between this production and distribution of wealth bring about?

6. According to the author, how do the people who distribute the money spend it?

7. What happens when the industrialists quarrel among themselves?

8. Why does the author believe that economic depressions are not natural phenomenas?

9. When there is a depression, crisis happens. What is capitalism's solution?

10. **DEFINE** each of the following words and **USE EACH IN A SENTENCE:**

    a. exploitation

    b. amnesty

    c. intolerable

    d. philanthropic

    e. impregnable

QUIZ—ARRIVAL AT MANZANAR

1. At the opening of the story, what type of neighborhood did the family live in? Why did the author's mother move them to Terminal Island?

2. Why did her mother have to work, where did she work, and at what times?

    a.

    b.

    c.

3. Why was the author so frightened after the family moved to Terminal Island?

4. Why did the Navy decide to clear Terminal Island?

5. What did the author's mother do with her good china? Why?

6. What had happened to the author's father and where was he?

7. Why was the author full of excitement the day they left L.A. for Manzanar?

8. What food were they served the first night? Why did they hate it? Why didn't they complain?

    a.

    b.

    c.

9. Why did the author's sister and her husband leave to go to Idaho?

10. **DEFINE** each of the following words and **USE EACH IN A SENTENCE:**

    a. abate

    b. inedible

    c. uncouth

    d. ghetto

    e. patriarch

QUIZ—THE WAYS OF MEETING OPPRESSION

1. Dr. King asserts that there are three characteristic ways people deal with oppression. If a person passively accepts an unjust system, what does he or she do with that system?

2. What does the author call a person who passively accepts this system?

3. How is acquiescence interpreted by the oppressor?

4. Another way to react is through violence. How is this viewed by Dr. King?

5. Tied in with violence is the old law of "an eye for an eye." How does this law leave everybody, according to the author?

6. Most importantly, how does violence end?

7. The third way is a balance between the first two. What is it?

8. Why is this third way difficult to achieve?

9. In order to work, the third way is not a struggle between people but a tension between what?

10. **DEFINE** each of the following words and **USE EACH IN A SENTENCE:**

   a. annihilate

   b. tacit

   c. synthesis

   d. sublime

   e. desolate

Quiz—American Indians:
Homeless in Their Own Homeland

1. How many American Indians are homeless on skid row?

2. How many American Indians live in Los Angeles, and of those, how many are one paycheck away from being homeless?

3. Why are many of the homeless American Indians reluctant to take shelter?

4. Why is there a conflict between American Indians and the U.S. capitalist system?

5. What is the goal of capitalist education for Indian people?

6. What have American Indians been taught about their communal ways?

7. What is the worst lesson being taught to American Indians?

8. What happens to homeless people who need help, for example, when they are in soup lines?

9. Name at least three ways that the U.S. government, the BIA, has "taken care" of the American Indian.

   a.

   b.

   c.

10. **DEFINE** each of the following words and **USE EACH IN A SENTENCE:**

    a. reluctant

    b. resurgence

    c. relocation

    d. indoctrination

    e. sobriety

157

Quiz—Who Is Your Mother?
Red Roots of White Feminism

1. At Laguna Pueblo in New Mexico what is an important question that is often asked?

2. Failure to know your position, history, and place in the scheme of things results in what?

3. Immigrants to America, according to the author, have a tendency to rid themselves of what kinds of ties?

4. How do these immigrants often see their ancestors or antecedents?

5. What do the Native Americans highly value?

6. This view (given in number 5 above) has the advantage of providing what?

7. In the past, there have been centuries of brutal effort by the American government, churches and businesses to do what to Native Americans?

8. The author believes that if American society embraced the traditions of various Native Americans, what would happen?

9. If we were to adopt these traditions, how would the view of women change?

10. **DEFINE** each of the following words and **USE EACH IN A SENTENCE:**

    a. antecedents

    b. matrilineal

    c. psychic

    d. alienated

    e. context

QUIZ—I WANT TO LIVE WITHOUT TROUBLE

1. During the time of French rule, what was the narrator considered to be?

2. What happened to the narrator when war broke out between China and Vietnam?

3. Why did the narrator think that America is really a paradise?

4. According to the narrator, what happens if people have no ideals, no attachments?

5. What does the narrator feel is "the bad thing about America"?

6. How does the narrator feel about the flag?

7. Why does the narrator think that Americans should have more children?

8. The narrator believes that technology has too much stress in the American educational system. What else should be given equal stress and why?

9. Why has the narrator become very cautious?

10. **DEFINE** each of the following words and **USE EACH IN A SENTENCE:**

   a. criterion

   b. capitalism

   c. individualistic

   d. communism

   e. aggression

VII. Suggested Multicultural Readings '98

We have included this selected bibliography of multicultural literature and resources because many teachers supplement their writing courses with occasional literary pieces. We intend this selection to act as a starting point for teachers searching for the occasional literary piece to use along with the essays in *Visions Across the Americas*. Dates may refer to the most recent edition of a text.

ANTHOLOGIES: MULTICULTURAL LITERATURE

Morga, Cherrie and Gloria Anzaldua.	*This Bridge Called My Back: Writing by Radical Women of Color*	(1983)
Payne, James Robert.	*Multi-Cultural American Biography*	(1987)
Reed, Ismael, Gundars Strads, and Shawn Wong.	*The Before Columbus Foundation Fiction Anthology: Selections from the American Book Awards, 1980-1990*	(1992)
	The Before Columbus Foundation Poetry Anthology: Selections from the American Book Awards, 1980-1990	(1992)
Simonson, Rick and Scott Walker.	*Multicultural Literacy: Opening the American Mind*	(1988)
Walker, Scott.	*Stories from the American Mosaic*	(1990)

RESOURCES: TEACHING IN A MULTICULTURAL CLASSROOM

Baker, Houston A.	*Three American Literatures: Essays in Chicano, Native American, and Asian American Literature for Teachers of American Literature*	(1982)
Banks, James A.	*Teaching Ethnic Studies*	(1991)
Banks, James A. and Cherry A. McGee.	*Multicultural Education: Issues and Perspectives*	(1989)
Garcia, Ricardo.	*Teaching in a Pluralistic Society*	(1991)
Perry, Theresa and James W. Fraser.	*Freedom's Plow: Teaching in the Multicultural Classroom*	(1993)
Ruoff, A., LoVonne Brown, and Jerry W. Ward, Jr.	*Redefining American Literary History*	(1990)
Trimmer, Joseph and Tilly Warnock.	*Understanding Others: Cultural and Cross-Cultural Studies and the Teaching of Literature*	(1992)

NATIVE AMERICAN LITERATURE

BACKGROUND AND ANTHOLOGIES:

Allen, Paula Gunn.	*Studies in American Indian Literature*	(1983)
	As Long as the River Flows: The Stories of Nine Native Americans (with Patricia Clark)	(1996)
Astrov, Margot.	*American Indian Prose and Poetry: An Anthology*	(1972)

Bird, Gloria.	*Dancing on the Rim of the World: An Anthology of Contemporary Northwest Native American Writing*	(1990)
Blackburn, T. C.	*December's Child: A Book of Chumash Oral Narratives*	(1975)
Brant, Beth.	*A Gathering of Spirit*	(1989)
Bruchac, Joseph.	*Songs from This Earth on Turtle's Back: Contemporary American Indian Poetry*	(1983)
Clark, Ella.	*Indian Legends from the Northern Rockies*	(1966)
Dorris, Michael.	*A Guide to Research on North American Indians*	(1983)
Eagle/Walking Turtle.	*Indian American*	(1989)
Hobson, Geary.	*The Remembered Earth: An Anthology of Contemporary Native-American Literature*	(1979)
Lestley, Craig.	*Talking Leaves: Contemporary Native American Short Stories*	(1991)
Niatum, Duane.	*Harper's Anthology of 20th Century Native American Poetry*	(1988)
Sarris, Greg.	*Keeping Slug Woman Alive: A Holistic Approach to American Indian Texts.*	(1993)
Turner, Frederick.	*The Portable North American Reader*	(1977)
Velie, Alan R.	*American Indian Literature: An Anthology*	(1979)
Visenor, Gerald.	*Native American Literature: A Brief Introduction and Anthology*	(1995)
Waters, Anna Lee.	*The Spirit of Native America: Beauty and Mysticism in American Indian Art*	(1989)
Wiget, Andrew.	*Critical Essays on Native American Literature*	(1985)

FICTION AND NONFICTION:

Allen, Paula Gunn.	*The Woman Who Owned the Shadows*	(1983)
	The Sacred Hoop: Recovering the Feminine in American Indian Traditions	(1986)
	Spider Woman's Granddaughters	(1990)
	Grandmothers of the Light: A Medicine Woman's Sourcebook	(1992)
Bennett, Kay.	*The Changing Woman Story*	(1964)
Carter, Forrest.	*Education of Little Tree*	(1976)
Cook-Lynn, Elizabeth.	*The Power of Horses and Other Stories*	(1990)

Deloria, Vine, Jr.	*Custer Died for Your Sins*	(1969)
	We Talk, You Listen	(1970)
	Frank Waters: Man and Mystic	(1993)
	God Is Red: A Native American View of Religion	(1993)
Dorris, Michael.	*A Yellow Raft in Blue Water*	(1987)
	A Broken Cord	(1989)
	The Crown of Columbus (Co-author)	(1991)
	Working Men: Stories	(1994)
	Paper Trails: Essays	(1995)
	Cloud Chamber: A Novel	(1997)
Erdrich, Louise.	*The Beet Queen*	(1986)
	Tracks	(1988)
	The Crown of Columbus (Co-author)	(1991)
	The Bingo Palace	(1994)
	Love Medicine	(1994)
	Tales of Burning Love: A Novel	(1996)
Harjo, Joy.	*In Mad Love, and War*	(1990)
Least Heat Moon, William.	*Blue Highways*	(1982)
	PrairyErth	(1991)
Momaday, N. Scott.	*House Made of Dawn*	(1968)
	The Way to Rainy Mountain	(1969)
	The Ancient Child	(1989)
	In the Presence of the Sun	(1992)
	The Man Made of Words	(1997)
Mourning Dove (Humushuma)	*Coyote Stories*	(1990)
Neihardt, John.	*Black Elk Speaks*	(1932)
Sarris, Greg.	*Mabel McKay: Weaving the Dream*	(1994)
	Grand Street	(1995)
Silko, Leslie M.	*The Man to Send Rain Clouds*	(1973)
	Ceremony	(1977)
	The Almanac of the Dead	(1991)
	Yellow Woman and a Beauty of the Spirit: Essays on Native American Life Today	(1996)
	Gardens in the Dunes: A Novel	(1997)
Vizenor, Gerald.	*Interior Landscapes*	(1990)
Walters, Anna Lee.	*The Sun Is Not Merciful*	(1985)

Welch, James.	*Winter in the Blood*	(1974)
	The Death of Jim Lonely	(1981)
	Fools Crow	(1986)

POETRY:

Allen, Paula Gunn.	*Life Is a Fatal Disease: New and Selected Poems, 1962–1995*	(1996)
Carroll Arnett/Gogisgi.	*Rounds*	(1982)
Blue Cloud, Peter.	*Coyote and Friends*	(1976)
	Back Then Tomorrow	(1978)
	White Corn Sister	(1979)
	Elderly Flute Song	(1982)
	Clans of Many Nations: New and Selected Poems, 1969–1994	(1997)
Erdrich, Louise.	*Jacklight*	(1984)
	Baptism of Desire	(1989)
Harjo, Joy.	*The Last Song*	(1973)
	What Moon Drove Me to This	(1980)
	She Had Some Horses	(1983)
	In Mad Love, and War	(1990)
Momaday, N. Scott.	*Angle of Geese and Other Poems*	(1974)
	The Gourd Dancer	(1976)
Nitatum, Duane.	*Carriers of the Dream Wheel*	(1975)
Ortiz, Simon.	*Going for the Rain*	(1976)
	From Sand Creek	(1981)
	Woven Stone	(1992)
	After and Before the Lightning	(1994)
Rose, Wendy.	*Hopi Roadrunner Dancing*	(1973)
	Builder Kachina: A Homegoing Cycle	(1979)
	Lost Cooper	(1980)
	Halfbreed Chronicles	(1984)
	Going to War with My Relatives: New and Selected Poems	(1993)
	Bone Dance: New and Selected Poems, 1965–1993	(1994)
Silko, Leslie M.	*Storyteller*	(1975)
Welch, James.	*Riding the Earthboy 40*	(1976)
Woody, Elizabeth.	*Hand into Stone*	(1988)
Young Bear, Ray A.	*Winter of the Salamander*	(1980)

HISPANIC AMERICAN LITERATURE

BACKGROUND AND ANTHOLOGIES:

Bryan, Ryan. Ed.	*Hispanic Writers: A Selection from Contemporary Authors*	(1991)
Bruce-Novoa, Juan D.	*Chicano Authors*	(1980)
Gonzalez, Ray.	*Currents from the Dancing River: Contemporary Latino Fiction, Nonfiction, and Poetry*	(1994)
Huerta, Jorge A.	*Chicano Theater: Themes and Forms*	(1982)
Poey, Delia and Virgil Suarez.	*Iguana Dreams: New Latino Fiction*	(1992)
Kanellos, Nicolas.	*Short Fiction by Hispanic Writers of the United States*	(1991)
	Hispanic Theater in the United States	(1984)
	A History of Hispanic Theater in the United States	(1990)
Martinez, Julio A. and Francisco A. Lomeli.	*Chicano Literature: A Reference Guide*	(1995)
Sommers, Joseph and Tomas Ybarra-Frausto.	*Modern Chicano Writers: A Collection of Critical Essays*	(1979)
Soto, Gary.	*Pieces of the Heart: New Chicano Fiction*	(1993)
Tatum, Charles M.	*A Selected and Annotated Bibliography of Chicano Studies*	(1979)
	New Chicana/Chicano Writing 1	(1992)
	New Chicana/Chicano Writing 2	(1992)

FICTION AND NONFICTION:

Alvarez, Julia.	*How the Garcia Girls Lost Their Accents*	(1992)
	In the Time of the Butterflies	(1995)
	Yo!	(1997)
Anaya, Rudolfo.	*Bless Me Ultima*	(1972)
	Heart of Aztlan	(1976)
	Tortuga	(1979)
	The Silence of the Llano	(1982)
	A Chicano in China	(1986)
Acosta, Oscar Zeta.	*The Autobiography of a Brown Buffalo*	(1972)
	The Revolt of the Cockroach People	(1976)
Anzaldua, Gloria.	*Borderlands/El Frontera*	(1987)
Arias, Ron.	*The Road to Tamazunchale*	(1975)

Azuela, Mariano.	*Two Novels of Mexico: The Flies and the Bosses*	(1956)
	The Underdogs	(1986)
Barrio, Raymond.	*The Plum Plum Pickers*	(1969)
Candelaria, Nash.	*Not by the Sword*	(1982)
	The Day the Cisco Kid Shot John Wayne	(1990)
	Leonor Park	(1991)
Castaneda, Carlos.	*The Teaching of Don Juan: A Yaqui Way of Knowledge*	(1968)
	Journey to Ixtlan	(1973)
	Tales of Power	(1975)
	Fire from Within	(1984)
Castillo, Ana.	*The Mixpuiahuala Letters*	(1986)
	Sapognia	(1989)
	Far from God	(1994)
	Massacre of the Dreamers: Essays on Xicanisma	(1995)
	Loverboys: Stories	(1996)
Chavez, Denise.	*The Last of the Menu Girls*	(1987)
	Face of an Angel	(1994)
Cisneros, Sandra.	*The House on Mango Street*	(1983)
	The Holy Night	(1991)
	Woman Hollering Creek	(1991)
Cofer, Judith Ortiz.	*The Line of the Sun*	(1989)
Galarza, Ernesto.	*Barrio Boy*	(1971)
García, Cristina.	*Dreaming in Cuban*	(1992)
Garcia, Lionel G.	*A Shroud in the Family*	(1987)
	Hardscrub	(1990)
Gómez-Peña, Guillermo	*Warrior for Gringostroka*	(1993)
	The New World Border	(1996)
	Temple of Confessions: Mexican Beasts and Living Saints	(1997)
Gonzalez, Genaro.	*Rainbow's End*	(1988)
Hijuelos, Oscar.	*Our House in the Lost World*	(1983)
	The Mambo Kings Play Songs of Love	(1990)
	Mr. Ive's Christmas: A Novel	(1996)
	The 14 Sisters of Emilio Montez O'Brien: A Novel	(1996)
Hinojosa-Smith, Rolando.	*Becky and Her Friends*	(1990)
Islas, Arturo.	*The Rain God*	(1984)
	Migrant Souls	(1990)

Martinez, Victor.	*Parrot in the Oven: Mi Vida: A Novel*	(1996)
Ponce, Helen.	*Taking Control*	(1987)
Portillo, Trambley Estela.	*Rain of Scorpions and Other Writings*	(1975)
	Trini	(1986)
Rios, Alberto Alvaro.	*The Iguana Killer: Twelve Stories of the Heart*	(1984)
	Pig Cookies and Other Stories	(1995)
Rivera, Thomas.	*"...Y no se lo trago la tierra"*	(1971)
Rodriguez, Luis J.	*Always Running: La Vida Loca: Gang Days in L.A.*	(1994)
	America Is Her Name	(1997)
Rodriguez, Richard.	*The Hunger of Memory*	(1982)
	Mexico's Children	(1991)
	Days of Obligation: An Argument with My Mexican Father	(1993)
Soto, Gary.	*Living up the Street*	(1985)
	California Childhood (Editor)	(1988)
	A Summer Life	(1990)
	Baseball in April	(1990)
	Pacific Crossings	(1991)
	Taking Sides	(1991)
	Crazy Weekend	(1994)
	Buried Onions	(1997)
Thomas, Piri.	*Down These Mean Streets*	(1967)
	Savior, Savior Hold My Hand	(1972)
	Stories from El Barrio	(1978)
Ulibarri, Sabine R.	*Mi abuela famaba puros y otros cuentos de Tierra Amarilla/My Grandmother Smokes Cigars: and Other Stories of Tierra Amarilla*	(1977)
	Primeros Encuentros/First Encounters	(1982)
	Governor Glu Glu and Other Stories	(1988)
	El Condor and Other Stories	(1990)
	Kissing Cousins: 1000 Words Common to English and Spanish	(1991)
	The Best of Sabine R. Ulibarri: Selected Stories (Paso Por Aqui)	(1993)
Vasquez, Richard.	*Chicano*	(1970)
Villarreal, José Antonio.	*Pocho*	(1959)
	The Fifth Horseman	(1974)
	Clemente Chacon	(1984)

Villaseñor, Victor.	*Macho!*	(1973)
	Rain of Gold	(1991)
	Wild Steps of Heaven	(1996)
Viramontes, Helena Maria.	*The Moths*	(1985)
	Under the Feet of Jesus	(1995)

POETRY:

Alvarez, Julia.	*Homecoming*	(1996)
	The Other Side/El Otro Lado	(1995)
Baca, Jimmy Santiago.	*Martin and Meditation of the South Valley*	(1987)
	Black Mesa Poems	(1989)
	Working in the Dark: Reflections of a Poet Working in the Barrio	(1994)
	In the Way of the Sun	(1997)
Castillo, Ana.	*Otro Canto*	(1977)
	The Invitation	(1979)
	Women Are Not Roses	(1984)
	My Father Was a Toltec	(1988)
Cervantes, Lorna D.	*Emplumada*	(1981)
	From the Cables of Genocide: Poems on Love and Hunger	(1991)
Cisneros, Sandra.	*Bad Boys*	(1980)
	My Wicked, Wicked Ways	(1988)
Cruz, Victor Hernandez.	*Snaps*	(1969)
	Mainland	(1973)
	Tropicalization	(1976)
	By Lingual Wholes	(1982)
	Rhythm, Content, and Flavor: New and Selected Poems	(1989)
	Red Beans	(1991)
Hernandez, Inéz.	*Con Razon, Corazon: Poetry*	(1977)
Herrera, Juan Felipe.	*Rebozos of Love*	(1974)
	Exiles of Desire	(1983)
	Night in Tunisia	(1985)
	Facegames	(1987)
	Love After the Riots	(1996)
	Mayan Drifter: Chicano Poet in the Lowlands of America	(1997)
	Laughing Out Loud, I Fly: A Caracajadas Yo Vuelo	(1998)

Martinez, Victor.	*Caring for a House*	(1992)
Mora, Pat.	*Chants*	(1984)
	Borders	(1986)
	Communion	(1991)
	Agua Santa: Holy Water	(1995)
Moraga, Cherrie.	*Loving in the War Years*	(!885)
Rios, Alberto Alvaro.	*Whispering to Fool the Wind*	(1982)
Robles, Margarita Luna.	*A Night in Tunisia*	(1990)
Rodriguez, Luis J.	*Poems Across the Pavement*	(1989)
	The Concrete River	(1991)
Salinas, Marta.	*Cuentos Chicanos*	(1984)
Salinas, Luis Omar.	*The Day of Sadness: Selected Poems*	(1985)
Santayana, George.	*The Last Puritan*	(1936)
	The Poet's Testament	(1953)
Soto, Gary.	*The Elements of San Joaquin*	(1977)
	Fire in My Hands	(1977)
	The Tales of Sunlight	(1978)
	Mexican Woman	(1979)
	Father Is a Pillow Tied to a Broom	(1980)
	Where Sparrows Work Hard	(1981)
	Black Hair	(1985)
	Who Will Know Us?	(1990)
Ulibarri, Sabine.	*Tierra Amarilla*	(1964)
	My Grandma Smoked Cigars	(1977)

DRAMA:

Machado, Eduardo.	*Broken Eggs*	(1984)
Morton, Carlos.	*Johnny Tenorio and Other Plays*	(1991)
Portillo, Trambley Estela.	*The Day of the Swallows*	(1976)
Sanchez-Scott, Milcha.	*Latina*	(1980)
	Dog Lady	(1984)
	Evening Star	(1988)
	The Architect Piece	(1991)
Valdez, Luis Miguel.	*The Shrunken Head of Pancho Villa*	(1963)
	Los Vendidos	(1967)
	Actos: El Teatro Campesino	(1971)
	Dark Root of a Scream	(1973)
	Mythology	(1976)
	Zoot Suit	(1978)

AFRICAN AMERICAN LITERATURE

BACKGROUND AND ANTHOLOGIES:

Abrahams, Robert D.	*African Folktales: Traditional Stories of the Black World*	(1983)
Baker, Houston A., Jr.	*The Journey Back*	(1980)
	Blues, Ideaology, and the Afro-American Literature	(1985)
	Modernism and the Harlem Renaissance	(1989)
Bell, Bernard W.	*The Afro-American Novel and its Tradition*	(1987)
Busby, Margaret.	*Daughters of Africa: An International Anthology*	(1992)
Christian, Barbara.	*Black Women Novelists: The Development of a Tradition*	(1980)
Evans, Mari.	*Black Women Writers*	(1984)
Fisher, Dexter and Robert B. Stepto.	*Afro-American Literature: The Reconstruction on Instruction*	(1978)
Goss, Linda and Martin Barnes.	*Talk That Talk: An Anthology of African-American Storytelling*	(1989)
Major, Clarence.	*Calling the Wind: 20th Century African-American Short Stories*	(1993)
McMillan, Terry.	*Breaking Ice: An Anthology of Contemporary African-American Writers*	(1990)
Tate, Claudia.	*Black Women Writers at Work*	(1983)
Walker, Mary Helen.	*Invented Lives: Narratives of Black Women 1860–1960*	(1987)

FICTION AND NONFICTION:

Angelou, Maya.	*I Know Why the Caged Bird Sings*	(1969)
	All God's Children Need Traveling Shoes	(1986)
	I Shall Not Be Moved	(1990)
	Wouldn't Take Nothing for My Journey Now	(1993)
Anza, Tina McElroy.	*Baby of the Family*	(1989)
	Ugly Ways	(1993)
Baldwin, James.	*Go Tell It on the Mountain*	(1953)
	Giovanni's Room	(1956)
	Another Country	(1962)
	Going to Meet the Man	(1965)
	If Beale St. Could Talk	(1974)
	Just Above My Head	(1979)
	The Price of the Ticket: Collected Nonfiction 1948–1985	(1985)
	The Evidence of Things Not Seen	(1985)

Bambara, Toni Cade.	*The Black Woman*	(1970)
	Gorilla, My Love	(1972)
	The Sea Birds Are Still Alive: Collected Stories	(1977)
	The Salt Eaters	(1980)
	Deep Sightings and Rescue Missions: Fiction, Essays, and Conversations	(1996)
Cartiér, Xam.	*Be-Bop, Re-Bop*	(1987)
	Muse-Echo Blues	(1991)
Chesnutt, Charles Waddell.	*The Conjure Woman*	(1899)
	The House Behind the Cedars	(1900)
	The Marrow of Tradition	(1901)
Ellison, Ralph.	*Invisible Man*	(1952)
Gaines, Ernest J.	*The Autobiography of Miss Jane Pitman*	(1976)
	A Gathering of Old Men	(1983)
	A Lesson Before Dying	(1993)
Giovanni, Nikki.	*A Dialogue: James Baldwin and Nikki Giovanni*	(1973)
	Sacred Cows ... and Other Edibles	(1988)
	Racism 101	(1995)
Haley, Alex.	*Roots*	(1976)
Hughes, Langston.	*Laughing to Keep from Crying*	(1935)
	The Big Sea	(1940)
Hurston, Zora Neale.	*Dust Tracks on a Road*	(1932)
	Jonah's Gourd Vine	(1934)
	Mules and Men	(1935)
	Their Eyes Were Watching God	(1937)
	Moses, Man of the Mountain	(1939)
Kincaid, Jamaica.	*Annie John*	(1985)
	Lucy	(1991)
	At the Bottom of the River	(1992)
	The Autobiography of My Mother	(1996)
King, Martin Luther, Jr.	*Stride Toward Freedom*	(1958)
	A Testament of Hope: The Essential Writing and Speeches of Martin Luther King, Jr. (J. M. Washington, Ed.)	(1991)
Malcolm X.	*The Autobiography of Malcolm X*	(1964)
Marshall, Paule.	*Brown Girl, Brown Stones*	(1981)
	The Chosen Place, The Timeless People	(1984)
	Praisesong for the Window	(1990)
	Daughters	(1992)

Mathabane, Mark.	*Kaffir Boy*	(1986)
	Kaffir Boy in America	(1989)
McMillan, Terry.	*Mama*	(1987)
	Disappearing Acts	(1989)
	Waiting to Exhale	(1992)
	How Stella Got Her Groove Back	(1996)
McPherson, James Alan.	*Elbow Room*	(1987)
Morrison, Toni.	*The Bluest Eye*	(1970)
	Sula	(1973)
	Song of Solomon	(1977)
	Tar Baby	(1981)
	Beloved	(1985)
	Jazz	(1992)
Mowry, Jesse.	*Way Past Cool*	(1992)
	Six Out Seven	(1993)
Naylor, Gloria.	*The Women of Brewster Place*	(1982)
	Linden Hills	(1985)
	Mama Day	(1988)
	Bailey's Cafe	(1992)
Reed, Ishmael.	*God Made Alaska for the Indians*	(1982)
	Last Days of Louisiana Red	(1982)
	Writin' is Fightin': Thirty-Seven Years of Boxing on Paper	(1988)
	Mumbo Jumbo	(1989)
	Airing Dirty Laundry	(1993)
Shange, Ntozake.	*Sassafrass, Cypress, and Indigo*	(1982)
	Betsey Brown	(1985)
	The Love Space Demands: A Continuing Saga	(1992)
	Liliani: Resurrection of the Daughter	(1995)
Toomer, Jean.	*Cane*	(1923)
Walker, Alice.	*The Third Life of Grace Copeland*	(1970)
	Meridian	(1976)
	You Can't Keep a Good Woman Down	(1981)
	The Color Purple	(1982)
	The Temple of My Familiar	(1989)
	Possessing the Secret of Joy	(1993)
	The Same River Twice: Honoring the Difficult	(1996)

Walker, Margaret.	*For My People*	(1942)
	Jubilee	(1966)
Wideman, John Edgar.	*Philadelphia Fire*	(1990)
	Fever	(1990)
	Brothers and Keepers	(1995)
	The Cattle Killing	(1996)
Williams, John.	*The Man Who Cried I Am*	(1985)
Wright, Richard.	*Native Son*	(1940)
	Black Boy	(1945)
Young, Al.	*Sitting Pretty*	(1986)
	Seduction by Light	(1988)
	Drowning in the Sea of Love: Musical Memoirs	(1995)

POETRY:

Angelou, Maya.	*And Still I Rise*	(1978)
	Poems, Maya Angelou, Four Books	(1986)
	On the Pulse of Morning	(1993)
	Phenomenal Women: Four Poems Celebrating Women	(1995)
Baraka, Imamu Amiri.	*Black Magic: Poetry 1961-1967*	(1967)
	Selected Poetry of Imamu Amiri Baraka/Leroi Jones	(1979)
Brooks, Gwendolyn.	*A Street in Bronzeville*	(1945)
	Annie Allen	(1949)
	The Bean Eaters	(1960)
	In the Mecca	(1968)
	Family Portraits	(1971)
	Blacks (Selected Poems)	(1991)
Clifton, Lucille.	*Good Times*	(1969)
	Good Woman: Poems and a Memoir, 1969-1980	(1987)
	Next: New Poems	(1987)
	Quilting: Poems 1987-1990	(1991)
	The Book of Light	(1993)
Cullen, Countee.	*Color*	(1925)
	Copper Sun	(1927)
Dove, Rita.	*Selected Poems*	(1993)
Dunbar, Paul Laurence.	*The Complete Poems*	(1913)
Evans, Mari.	*I Look at Me*	(1974)
	A Dark and Splendid Mass	(1992)

Giovanni, Nikki.	*Selected Poems*	(1996)
Hughes, Langston.	*The Panther and the Lash: Poems of Our Times*	(1951)
	Selected Poems	(1959)
	Don't Turn Your Back	(1970)
Jordon, June.	*Some Changes*	(1971)
	New Days: Poems of Exile and Return	(1973)
	Selected Poems of June Jordon: Things That I Do in the Dark	(1977)
Knight, Etheridge.	*Born of Woman: New and Selected Poems*	(1980)
	The Essential Etheridge Knight	(1986)
Lockett, Reginald.	*Good Times and No Bread*	(1978)
	Where the Birds Sing Bass	(1994)
Lorde, Audre.	*Chosen Poems, Old and New*	(1982)
	Our Dead Behind Us: Poems	(1986)
Reed, Ishmael.	*Catechism of a Neo-American*	(1969)
	Japanese By Spring	(1996)
Sanchez, Sonia.	*Homegirls and Handgrenades*	(1984)
	I've Been a Woman: Selected Poems	(1985)
	Friend	(1995)
	Does Your House Have Lions?	(1997)
Shange, Ntozake.	*for colored girls who had considered suicide/when the rainbow is enuf*	(1974)
	Ridin' the Moon in Texas: Word Paintings	(1987)
Troupe, Quincy.	*Embryo*	(1972)
	Weather Reports	(1991)
Walker, Alice.	*Her Blue Body Everything We Know: Earthling Poems 1965–1990 Complete*	(1993)
Young, Al.	*Heaven: Collected Poems 1958–1988*	(1989)

ASIAN AMERICAN LITERATURE

BACKGROUND AND ANTHOLOGIES:

Chin, Frank.	*Aiieeeee! An Anthology of Asian American Writers*	(1974)
	The Big Aiieeee! An Anthology of Chinese American and Japanese American Literature	(1991)
Hamilton-Merritt, Jane.	*Tragic Mountains: The Hmong, The Americans, and the Secret War*	(1993)

Hagedorn, Jessica.	*Charlie Chan Is Dead: An Anthology of Contemporary Asian American Fiction*	(1993)
Hongo, Garrett.	*The Open Boat: Asian American Poetry*	(1993)
	Under Western Eyes: Personal Essays for Asian Americans	(1995)
Hosokawa, Bill.	*Nisei: The Quiet Americans*	(1969)
Hsu, Francis L. K.	*The Challenge of the American Dream: The Chinese in the United States*	(1971)
Huong, Patricia Nguyen.	*Language in Vietnamese Society: Some Articles by Nguyen Dinh-Hoa*	(1990)
Lukes, Timothy J.	*Japanese Legacy: Farming and Community Life in California's Santa Clara*	(1985)
Lydon, Sandy.	*Chinese Gold: The Chinese in the Monterey Bay Region*	(1985)
Mirikitani, Janice, James Masao Mitsui, Jerrold Asao, Hirua Hirasu.	*The Hawks Well: A Collection of Japanese American Art and Literature*	(1987)
Tachili, Amy.	*Roots: An Asian American Reader*	(1971)
Weglyn, Michi.	*Years of Infamy: The Untold Story of America's Concentration Camps*	(1976)
Yep, Laurence.	*Asian Dragons: 25 Asian American Voices*	(1995)

FICTION AND NONFICTION:

Akutagawa, Ryanosuke.	*Rashomon and Other Stories*	(1952)
Aruego, Jose.	*A Crocodile's Tale: A Philippine Folk Story*	(1975)
Bulosan, Carlos.	*The Laughter of My Father*	(1942)
	America Is in the Heart	(1977)
	If You Want to Know What We Are: A Carlos Bulosan Reader	(1983)
Chin, Frank.	*The Chickencoop Chinaman and the Year of the Dragon: Two Plays*	(1981)
	Donald Duk	(1991)
	Gunga Din Highway: A Novel	(1995)
Dinh, Tran Van.	*Blue Dragon, White Tiger: A Tet Story*	(1983)
Divakaruni, Chitra.	*Arranged Marriage*	(1995)
Hagedorn, Jesica.	*Dangerous Music*	(1975)
	Dogeaters	(1990)
	Danger and Beauty	(1993)
	The Gangster of Love	(1996)
Hau, On-Nhu.	*The Complaints of an Odalisque*	(1967)

Hongo, Garrett.	*Volcano: A Memoir of Hawaii*	(1995)
Hom, Marlon.	*Songs of Gold Mountain: Cantonese Rhymes from San Francisco Chinatown*	(1987)
Houston, Jeanne Wakatsuki.	*Farewell to Manzanar*	(1973)
	One Can Think About Life After the Fish Is in the Canoe: Beyond Manzanar	(1988)
Jen, Gish.	*Typical American*	(1991)
Kamani, Ginu.	*Jungle Girl*	(1995)
Kingston, Maxine Hong.	*The Woman Warrior: Memories of a Girlhood Among Ghosts*	(1975)
	China Men	(1981)
	Tripmaster Monkey	(1987)
	Hawaii One Summer	(1987)
Kogawa, Joy.	*Obasan: A Novel*	(1982)
Lee, Chang Rae.	*Native Speaker*	(1995)
Lee, Gus (Mein-Sun).	*China Boy*	(1991)
	Honor and Duty	(1994)
	Tiger's Tail	(1997)
Masumato, David Mas.	*Epitaph for a Peach*	(1995)
Meer, Ameena.	*Bombay Talkie*	(1994)
Mukherjee, Bharati.	*The Middleman and Other Stories*	(1988)
Mura, David.	*A Male Grief: Notes on Pornography and Addiction*	(1987)
	Turning Japanese: Memoirs of a Sansei	(1991)
Mori, Toshio.	*Yokohama, California*	(1949)
	The Chauvinist and Other Stories	(1979)
	The Woman from Hiroshima	(1979)
Ngan, Nguyen Ngoc.	*The Will of Heaven*	(1982)
Okada, John.	*The No-No Boy*	(1979)
Robles, Al.	*Looking for Ifugao Mountain*	(1977)
Sone, Monica.	*Nisei Daughter*	(1953)
Tan, Amy.	*The Joy Luck Club*	(1989)
	The Kitchen God's Wife	(1991)
	The Hundred Secret Senses	(1996)
Tanizaki, Junichiro.	*Some Prefer Nettles*	(1929)
	Arrowroot	(1930)
	The Makioka Sister	(1948)
	Childhood Years: A Memoir	(1988)
Vien, Minh.	*Saigon: The Unhealed Wound*	(1990)
Wong, Jade Snow.	*Fifth Chinese Daughter*	(1945)
	No Chinese Stranger	(1975)

Wong, Shawn.	*Homebase*	(1990)
	American Knees	(1995)
Yamada, Mitsuye.	*Desert Run: Poems and Stories*	(1988)
Yamamoto, Hisaye.	*Seventeen Syllables*	(1949)
	Yoneko's Earthquake: The Collected Stories	(1988)
Yep, Laurence.	*Dragonwings*	(1975)
	Hiroshima: A Novella	(1995)
Yoshikawa, Eiji.	*Musashi*	(1971)

POETRY:

Divakaruni, Chitra.	*The Reason for Nasturtiums*	(1990)
	Black Candle	(1991)
Hagedorn, Jessica.	*Pet Food and Tropical Apparitions*	(1981)
Hongo, Garrett.	*The River of Heaven*	(1988)
Inada, Lawson Fusao.	*Legends from Camp*	(1993)
Lee, Li-Young.	*Rose*	(1985)
Mirijitani, Janice.	*We, The Dangerous: New and Selected Poems*	(1996)
Mitsui, James Masao.	*Journal of the Sun*	(1974)
	Crossing the Phantom River	(1978)
	After the Long Train	(1986)
	From a 3-Cornered World: New and Selected Poems	(1997)
Mura, David.	*After We Lost Our Way*	(1989)
Suknaski, Andrew.	*Wood Mountain Poems*	(1976)
Tsui, Kitty.	*The Words of a Woman Who Breathes Fire*	(1983)
Yamada, Mitsuye.	*Yamada's Camp Notes*	(1976)

MORE FICTION, NONFICTION AND POETRY FROM THE AMERICAS AND BEYOND

Allen, Woody. (United States)	*Getting Even*	(1971)
	Without Feathers	(1975)
	Side Effects	(1980)
Allende, Isabel. (Chile/United States)	*Of Love and Shadows*	(1984)
	The House of the Spirits	(1985)
	Eva Luna	(1988)
	The Stories of Eva Luna	(1992)
	The Infinite Plan	(1994)
	Paula	(1995)

Allison, Dorothy. (United States)	*Bastard Out of Carolina*	(1992)
Alter, Stephen (Ed.).	*The Penguin Book of Modern Indian Short Stories*	(1989)
Amado, Jorge. (Brazil)	*Sea of the Dead*	(1936)
	Gabriella, Clove, and Cinnamon	(1958)
	Pen, Sword, Camisole	(1981)
	Showdown	(1988)
	The War of the Saints	(1995)
Atwood, Margaret. (Canada)	*The Edible Woman*	(1969)
	Bodily Harm	(1981)
Aveling, Harry.	*Contemporary Indonesian Poetry*	(1975)
Banerian, James.	*The Vietnamese Short Story Introduction*	(1982)
Behn, Harry (Ed.).	*Cricket Songs: Japanese Haiku*	(1964)
Borges, Jorge Luis. (Argentina)	*Fictions*	(1944)
	Labyrinths	(1962)
	The Aleph and Other Stories	(1970)
	Dr. Brodie's Report	(1972)
	Poetry: *The Gold of the Tigers: Selected Later Poems*	(1972)
Bowas, Geoffrey (Ed.)	*The Penguin Book of Japanese Verse*	(1964)
Burgess, Anthony. (British)	*A Clockwork Orange*	(1962)
	Any Old Iron	(1989)
Campbell, Joseph. (United States)	*The Hero with a Thousand Faces*	(1949)
Castellanos, Rosario. (Mexico)	*A Rosario Castellanos Reader*	(1988)
	Another Way to Be: Selected Works	(1990)
Cather, Willa. (United States)	*The Troll Garden and Selected Stories*	(1905)
	My Antonia, A Lost Lady	(1918)
	Youth and the Bright Medusa	(1920)
	Death Comes for the Archbishop	(1927)
Chopin, Kate. (United States)	*The Awakening*	(1899)
Cliff, Michelle. (Jamaica/United States)	*Abeng*	(1984)
	The Land of Look Behind: Prose and Poetry	(1985)
	No Telephone to Heaven	(1987)
	Free Enterprise	(1993)
	Bodies of Water	(1996)

Cooper, Arthur (Trans).	*Li Po and Tu Fu*	(1988)
Cortazar, Julio.	*Hopscotch*	(1963)
(Argentina)	*The End of the Game*	(1965)
	We Love Glenda So Much	(1980)
	Blow Up and Other Stories	(1985)
	Unreasonable Hours	(1995)
Dario, Ruben.	*Selected Poems*	(1965)
(Nicaragua)	*Cuentos Completos*	(1994)
	Azul/Blue	(1996)
Didion, Joan.	*Slouching Towards Bethlehem*	(1966)
(United States)	*Play It As It Lays*	(1970)
	Salvador	(1983)
	Democracy	(1984)
	The Living	(1992)
Do, Nguyen. (Vietnam)	*Kim Van Kieu* (Le-Xuan-Thuy, Trans.)	(1960)
Dostoevsky, Fyodor.	*Crime and Punishment*	(1866)
(Russia)	*The Brothers Karamazov*	(1886)
Faulkner, William.	*The Sound and the Fury*	(1929)
(United States)	*As I Lay Dying*	(1930)
Ferlinghetti, Lawrence.	*A Coney Island of the Mind*	(1958)
(United States)		
Forster, E. M.	*A Room with a View*	(1923)
(Britain)	*A Passage to India*	(1936)
Fuentes, Carlos.	*Masked Days*	(1954)
(Mexico/United States)	*The Death of Artemio Cruz*	(1962)
	Change of Skin	(1968)
	Where the Air Is Clear	(1971)
	Terra Nostra	(1975)
	Burnt Water	(1980)
	The Old Gringo	(1985)
	Christopher Unborn	(1989)
Graham, A. C. (Ed.).	*Poems of the Late T'ang*	(1988)
Márquez, Gabriel García.	*No One Writes to the Colonel*	(1968)
(Colombia/Mexico)	*and Other Stories*	
	One Hundred Years of Solitude	(1970)
	Leaf Storm and Other Stories	(1972)
	Innocent Erendira and Other Stories	(1978)
	Chronicle of a Death Foretold	(1981)
	Collected Stories	(1984)

Gilman, Charlotte Perkins. (United States)	*The Yellow Wallpaper and Other Stories*	(1891)
Golding William. (Britain)	*Lord of the Flies*	(1954)
Guterson, David. (United States)	*Snow Falling on Cedars*	(1995)
Heaney, Seamus. (Ireland)	*Selected Poems 1966–1987*	(1988)
	Seeing Things	(1991)
	The Spirit Level	(1997)
Heker, Lillian. (Argentina)	*Those Beheld the Burning Bush*	(1966)
	Las Peras del Mal	(1982)
	Zona de Clivage	(1988)
	The Stolen Party and Other Stories	(1994)
Heller, Joseph (United States)	*Catch 22*	(1955)
	Something Happened	(1966)
Hesse, Hermann. (Switzerland)	*Steppenwolf*	(1927)
	Narcissus and Goldmund	(1932)
	Magister Ludi (The Glass Bead Game)	(1943)
	Siddhartha	(1951)
	Journey to the East	(1956)
Huxley, Aldous. (Britain/United States)	*Brave New World*	(1932)
Huidobro, Vicente. (Chile)	*Altazor and Other Poems*	(1931)
Jackson, Shirley. (United States)	*The Lottery*	(1944)
	The Haunting of Hill House	(1959)
	We Have Always Lived in the Castle	(1962)
	The Magic of Shirley Jackson	(1966)
Joyce, James. (Ireland)	*Dubliners*	(1914)
	A Portrait of the Artist as a Young Man	(1916)
	Ulysses	(1922)
	Finnegan's Wake	(1939)
Kawabata, Yasunari. (Japan)	*The Izu Dancer*	(1926)
	Snow Country	(1937)
	Thousand Cranes	(1953)
	The Sound of the Mountain	(1954)
	Palm-of-the Hand Stories	(1964)
Kerouac, Jack. (United States)	*On the Road*	(1955)
	The Dharma Bums	(1958)
	Dr. Sax	(1959)

Kerouac, Jack. (United States)	*Lonesome Traveler*	(1960)
	Desolation Angels	(1965)
	Vanity of Duluoz	(1968)
Kafka, Franz. (Germany)	*The Metamorphosis*	(1915)
	The Trial	(1925)
	Amerika	(1927)
Kazuo, Ishiguro. (Britain)	*A Pale View of the Hills*	(1982)
	An Artist of the Floating World	(1986)
	Remains of the Day	(1990)
Keillor, Garrison. (United States)	*Happy to Be Here*	(1982)
	Lake Wobegon Days	(1985)
	Leaving Home: Lake Wobegon Stories	(1987)
	We Are Still Married	(1989)
	WLT: A Radio Romance	(1992)
Kim, So-un. (Korea)	*The Story Bag: A Collection of Korean Folktales*	(1955)
Komachi, Ono No and Izumi Shikibu. (Japan)	*The Ink Dark Moon* (Jane Hirshfield, Trans.)	(1988)
LaPuma, Salvatore. (United States)	*The Boys from Bensonhurst*	(1987)
Lawrence, D. H. (Britain)	*The Plumed Serpent*	(1926)
Laygo, Teresita (Ed.).	*Well of Time: Eighteen Short Stories from Philippine Contemporary Literature*	(1977)
Lee, Harper (United States)	*To Kill a Mockingbird*	(1960)
Le Guinn, Ursula. (United States)	*Left Hand of Darkness*	(1969)
	The Dispossessed	(1974)
LeSueur, Meridel. (United States)	*Ripening: Selected Works*	(1986)
Lopez, Barry. (United States)	*Desert Notes: Reflections in the Eye of a Raven*	(1976)
	River Notes: The Dance of the Herons	(1979)
	Of Wolves and Men	(1979)
	Arctic Dreams	(1985)
	Field Notes	(1995)
	Crossing Open Ground	(1989)
Mahfouz, Naguib. (Egypt)	*Midaq Alley*	(1947)
	The Thief and the Dogs	(1961)
	Miramar	(1967)
Malamud, Bernard. (United States)	*The Natural*	(1952)
	The Assistant	(1957)

Malamud, Bernard.	*The Fixer*	(1966)
(United States)	*God's Grace*	(1982)
Marti, Jose.	*Simple Lyrics*	(1991)
(Cuba)	*Jose Marti Reader*	(1997)
	Drama:	
Miller, Arthur.	*Death of a Salesman*	(1940)
(United States)	*The Crucible*	(1953)
	The Creation of the World	(1972)
Mishima, Yukio.	*The Sound of Waves*	(1956)
(Japan)	*Five Modern No Plays*	(1957)
	Temple of the Golden Pavilion	(1959)
	After the Banquet	(1963)
	The Sailor Who Fell from Grace with the Sea	(1963)
	Confessions of a Mask	(1968)
	Spring Snow	(1972)
	Runaway Horses	(1973)
	The Temple of Dawn	(1973)
	The Decay of the Angel	(1974)
Murasaki, Shikibu.	*The Tale of Genji*	(1010)
(Japan)		
Neruda, Pablo.	*Selected Poems*	(1972)
(Chile)	*Late and Posthumous Poems 1968-1974*	(1988)
Oates, Joyce Carol.	*Marriage, Infidelities, and Other Stories*	(1972)
(United States)	*Raven's Wing*	(1986)
	The Assignation	(1988)
	Marya: A Life	(1989)
Ogot, Grace.	*The Promised Land*	(1966)
(United States)	*The Land Without Thunder*	(1968)
Olsen, Tillie.	*Silences*	(1978)
(United States)		
O'Connor, Flannery.	*Wise Blood*	(1951)
(United States)	*The Complete Stories*	(1981)
Orwell, George. (Britain)	*Animal Farm*	(1946)
Palma, Ricardo. (Peru)	*Peruvian Traditions*	(1972)
Paz, Octavio.	*The Labyrinth of Solitude*	(1950)
(Mexico)	*Altering Current*	(1967)
	Configurations	(1971)
	A Draft of Shadows	(1972)
	Eagle or Sun?	(1976)

Paz, Octavio. (Mexico)	*The Monkey Grammarian*	(1981)
	A Tree Within	(1987)
	Convergences: Essays on Art and Literature	(1987)
	One Word to the Other	(1989)
	Poetry: *Early Poems 1935–1955*	(1973)
	The Collected Poems of Octavio Paz, 1957–1987	(1987)
Plath, Sylvia. (United States)	*The Bell Jar*	(1971)
Porter, Katherine Ann. (United States)	*Flowering Judas and Other Stories*	(1930)
	Pale Horse, Pale Rider	(1939)
	Ship of Fools	(1962)
Puig, Manuel. (Argentina)	*Kiss of the Spider Woman*	(1976)
	Pubis Angelical	(1979)
	Tropical Night Falling	(1993)
	Betrayed by Rita Hayward	(1996)
	Heartbreak Tango: A Serial	(1996)
Rexroth, Kenneth (Ed.).	*One Hundred More Poems from the Chinese*	(1971)
	One Hundred More Poems from the Japanese	(1974)
Rhys, Jean. (Welsh)	*Wide Sargasso Sea*	(1966)
Roethke, Theodore. (United States)	*Collected Poems of Theodore Roethke*	(1953)
Salinger, J. D. (United States)	*A Catcher in the Rye*	(1951)
Selzer, Richard. (United States)	*Confessions of a Knife*	(1979)
Simic, Charles. (United States)	*The World Doesn't End*	(1990)
Singer, Isaac Beshevis. (Yiddish/United States)	*The Collected Stories*	(1982)
	The Image and Other Stories	(1985)
Sontag, Susan. (United States)	*Illness as Metaphor*	(1978)
	A Susan Sontag Reader	(1982)
Soyinka, Wole. (Nigeria)	Drama: *The Trails of Brother Jero*	(1964)
	Death of the King's Horseman	(1975)
	Requiem for a Futurologist	(1985)
	Poetry: *A Shuttle in the Crypt*	(1972)

Stryk, Lucien and Takashi Ikemoto.	*Zen Poems of China and Japan*	(1973)
Tagore, Rabindranath. (India)	*The House Warming and Other Selected Writings*	(1965)
Telles, Lygia Fagundes. (Brazil)	*Tigrela and Other Stories*	(1977)
Téllez, Hernando. (Colombia)	*The Restless of the World*	(1943)
	Ashes to the Wind and Other Stories	(1946)
	Literature	(1951)
	In the Name of Confession	(1966)
Thoreau, Henry David. (United States)	*Walden*	(1854)
Hemingway, Ernest. (United States)	*The Old Man and the Sea*	(1952)
Tolstoy, Leo. (Russia)	*War and Peace*	(1869)
	The Death of Ivan Ilych	(1886)
Twain, Mark. (United States)	*The Adventures of Tom Sawyer*	(1876)
	Life on the Mississippi	(1883)
	Huckleberry Finn	(1885)
Tyler, Royall (Ed. & Trans.)	*Japanese Tales*	(1987)
Valenzuela, Luisa. (Argentina)	*Open Door*	(1988)
	The Censors	(1992)
	Lizard's Tail	(1992)
	Bedside Manners	(1995)
Vallejo, Cesar. (Peru)	*Black Heralds*	(1918)
	Spain: Let This Cup Pass from Me	(1938)
	Human Poems	(1938)
Vargas-Llosa, Mario. (Peru)	*The Time of the Hero*	(1963)
	The Greenhouse	(1966)
	Aunt Julia and the Scriptwriter	(1982)
	A Fish in Water: A Memoir	(1994)
	Death in the Andes	(1996)
Ventura, Michael. (United States)	*Shadow Dancing in the U.S.A.*	(1992)
	Letters at 3 AM	(1993)
Vonnegut, Kurt. (United States)	*Cat's Cradle*	(1963)
	Slaughterhouse Five	(1969)
	Breakfast of Champions	(1972)
	Jailbird	(1979)
Watson, Burton (Trans.).	*Kanshi: The Poetry of Ishikawa Jozan and Other Edo-Period Poets*	(1990)

Welty, Eudora. (United States)	*Collected Stories of Eudora Welty*	(1982)
West, Nathanael. (United States)	*Miss Lonelyhearts*	(1933)
	Day of the Locust	(1939)
Wharton, Edith. (United States)	*Ethan Frome*	(1911)
Whincup, Greg (Trans.).	*The Heart of Chinese Poetry*	(1987)
Wolfe, Tom. (United States)	*The Electric Kool-Aid Acid Test*	(1968)
	The Right Stuff	(1977)
	The Purple Decades: A Reader	(1984)
	Bonfire of the Vanities	(1987)
Woolfe, Virginia. (Britain)	*Jacob's Room*	(1922)
	Mrs. Dalloway	(1925)
	To the Lighthouse	(1927)
	A Room of One's Own	(1929)
	The Waves	(1931)
Xianliang, Zhang. (China)	*Half of Man Is Woman*	(1986)
Zamora, Daisy.	*Clean Slate: New and Selected Poems*	(1993)

BROWARD ESL PROGRAM
COMMUNITY COLLEGE
JUDSON A. SAMUELS
SOUTH CAMPUS
7200 HOLLYWOOD/PINES BOULEVARD
PEMBROKE PINES, FL 33024